# Pimp it Yourself!

Published by National Lampoon Press

National Lampoon, Inc. • 8228 Sunset Boulevard • Los Angeles • California • 90046 • USA American Stock Exchange: NLN

NATIONAL LAMPOON, NATIONAL LAMPOON PRESS and colophon are trademarks of National Lampoon

Pimp it yourself  /  by Dirty Mike, Jeremy Rode and SamSkillz  -- 1st ed.

p.  cm.

ISBN-10: 0-9788323-7-X

ISBN-13: 978-0-9788323-7-7

Book Design and Production by
JK NAUGHTON

Jacket design by
Sam McCay and Sam Elhag

Cover photography
© Photos.com and Daniel Sakow
Skull illustraton © Nopow I Dreamstime.com
Hand model: Rex Perez

PRINTED IN THE UNITED STATES OF AMERICA

1    3    5    7    9    10    8    6    4    2

OCTOBER  2007

WWW.NATIONALLAMPOON.COM

# Pimp it Yourself!

## By Dirty Mike & Jeremy Rode

# CONTENTS

# CRIB NOTES
## Interior Decorating

# FIGHTING STARVATION
## Cooking

# BOTTOMS UP
## Drinking

# THE WEEKEND
## Partying

# TOO MUCH TIME ON YOUR HANDS
## Fun & Games

# INTRODUCTION

Ever want to get off that couch and do something? Do you even have a couch? Look, we slack off and waste as much time as you, but I bet we impress way more chicks.

Check it. Do you even have any idea how badass a Laser Light Show makes a party? Let me tell you, really badass. This book will show you how to impress your friends and pimp the hell out of that hobbit-hole studio apartment you lay around in all day long - for pretty cheap and not too much effort. Except for the Beer Bottle Oil Lamp. That can get pretty expensive depending on how many things you accidentally light on fire.

Some projects in this book are just for fun, like a Water Balloon Launcher (we built this to use on National Lampoon when they threatened not to print this), but others are useful and will save you money, like Cardboard Furniture.

We think the Fatty-Detecting Doormat is key for any party, not because we're prejudiced, but because we only bought three bags of Sun Chips and a keg of light beer. Oh, and we also don't think threatening trespassers with our Foam Gun makes us horrible people.

The point is, we can't hook you up with someone to wrestle in your Mud Pit, try out your Traveling Stripper Pole, or break in your Vibrating Couch, but we can show you how to build those things.

Picture this: You and that girl-whose-name-you-can't-remember get back to your house from a movie. Your date walks in to see a glowing 40 Ounce Lava Lamp made out of a bottle of imported 1974 vintage Olde English. "I built that," you say smugly. You take another sip from your sleeve and then hang your Drink Dispensing Jacket on its hook.

While your date sits on the couch, you pour a couple beers from the Keg-o-rator and with a single remote, turn on some romantic Party Lighting. She calls you a "nerd" at first, but with the touch of another button your Vibrating Couch starts moving to the music.

You grill up some cheese sandwiches on an iron for dinner as she stares at the Giant Poster of Your Face on the wall.

That night, you shoot a potato through her window with a love-note wrapped around it. Deal closed. Good thing the Love Hammock you built holds two.

# DISCLAIMER

Hey, anything you do in this book could burn your house down. That's right, even the Ice Shot Glasses. It's your fault if your neighbor calls the cops on you or you lose your arm trying to build the Laser Light Show. Fuck it; just don't even try to do anything in the book.

Bikini Girl

# HOW TO READ THIS BOOK

## (Note: Requires knowledge of the English language)

Blue Box

Step Number

Red Arrow

**1** How-To instructions are in this book and numbered in blue boxes, except where they're not. But if you follow those directions, you should be able to build any of these inventions.

Red arrows point to important information. Sometimes text is highlighted.

Highlighted Text

Bikini girls holding signs appear periodically because we wanted to do a photoshoot with bikini girls holding signs.

Jeremy

In the speech bubbles, Jeremy will chime in with helpful hints on the building process. And Dirty Mike will be popping by to ask the really important questions (like, "How will a Pump-Action T-Shirt Cannon get me laid?").

You

Dirty Mike

Knowing you, Mr. Attention Deficit Disorder, you will probably flip to a random invention and immediately try to build it. We recommend you at least read the How-To instructions for the inventions you want to build, so you don't burn your house down (see: Disclaimer, two pages back).

And oh yeah, this book is brought to you by National Lampoon in conjunction with DrunkUniversity.com.

# ABOUT THE AUTHORS

We're two guys who sit on the couch all day: one watches TV, and the other invents a bunch of crap. Dirty Mike may live in a run-down pad, but with the help of his long-time buddy and world-class engineer, Jeremy Rode, even Dirty Mike learned how to live like a king on a pauper's budget.

Dirty Mike and Jeremy Rode have been friends for years, but they couldn't have turned out more different.

## Jeremy Rode

While pursuing a doctorate in electrical engineering, Jeremy spends all of his time dreaming up his next crazy invention to pimp his crib. This modern-day MacGyver has also written for textbooks, served as an expert witness in patent cases, and knows everything about everything. Just ask him.

Jeremy's answers to a random survey off the Internet.

> Q: Do you believe in love at first sight?
> A: Love is just a biochemical reaction that releases dopamine, noradrenalin and phenyl ethylamine in the brain, so obviously I believe in it. It's chemistry.
>
> Q: Do you consider yourself conceited?
> A: Only if by "conceited" you mean "fucking awesome."
>
> Q: What was your favorite TV show as a kid?
> A: *Bill Nye the Science Guy*. I loved pointing out his scientific mistakes.

# *Dirty Mike*

Dirty Mike is your stereotypical bachelor. He's always out of food, broke, and can't find his toothbrush. Mike is construction incompetent and prone to bodily injury. But he's also a stand up comedian, and an almost-pro baseball player who practices yoga in his spare time.

Dirty Mike's answers to a random survey off the Internet.

Q: What time do you wake up in the morning?
A: I haven't woken up in the "morning" in three years.

Q: What's your favorite drink?
A: Jack on the Rocks. I went to bartender school for a while, but got kicked out for practicing how to make a Jack on the Rocks ten too many times. I wanted to get it perfect.

Q: Now that you're a published author, what will you do with the fame and fortune?
A: What a convenient random question, Mr. Internet Survey. Probably get drunk.

Dirty Mike's Favorite Story About Jeremy
"My roommates kept accidentally breaking things around my house so I came up with a rule - don't break anything unless you can fix it. When I told Jeremy the rule he smashed my television with a bat. Then he fixed it."

# CONTRIBUTORS

DrunkUniversity.com is run by a bunch of highly-professional college-trained drinkers.

Sometimes they write stuff.

These guys helped make our book not suck.

## SamSkillz

Founder of several start-up companies, comedy writer, Photoshopper, million-dollar-plan concocter and 6th year college student.

Sam knows a little bit about everything and has taken three forms of martial arts.

He owns a horse named Elmer.

## Rex "Rexican" Perez

Founder and publisher of *The Kiss My Aztec* comedy newspaper of San Diego State University, and the barroom rag *Lush Magazine*...both of which are now defunct.

He has to drink at least five beers to fall asleep.

He lives in LA now so he thinks he's a hot shot.

## Evan "E-Dawg" Hoovler

Former Chief Editor of *The Koala* comedy newspaper of the University of California, San Diego, E-Dawg's jokes have been heard by over 10 million people.

He has spent a decade making a living by writing comedy for well-known franchises including The Spark, DrunkUniversity.com, and the N.T.N. television cable network.

# *Brad "B-rad" Kohlenberg*

"The Cute One," Brad is a former editor of *The Koala*, was published in Genome Research, received the first ever granted Cal-(IT)2 Bioinformatics Scholar Award, and was on TV that one time for like 5 seconds.

Currently he is working his ass off at a start-up software company in Silicon Valley.

He drew some stuff in this book.

## *Dune Murderous*

Rapper of the infamous band Defamation League, he brews his own beer, has been featured in *Hustler* magazine, has won music awards, and puts out club jams on an almost weekly basis.

Dune's hobbies include whiskey.

He drew some stuff too.

Photo Credit: Daniel Sakow
Awesome Credit: SamSkillz

## SPECIAL THANKS

We also want to thank all the following people who didn't help at all, but will have to buy a copy of this book because we put their name in it: George Lee Liddle III, Nick Sleezin', Khemicle Ali, Acacia Blair, Mako Polo, Zach Posner, Milkman, Bryan Barton, Elle A. Phant, J-Rhodes, The Rothman, Aaron Crayford, Marissa Crane, TylOr, Bear Paw, Davey G, Gil Shafir, Mary Carey, Jesse Grce, Beth Chapin, Anne McDermott, Steve Lui, Erik Kap, T-Bone, Kelly Goodnuff, Mike Sowers, Moximo, Melanie Rodgers, Daniel Watts, Legally Mike, Monica Rieder, Sara Jamshidi, Paula Koala, Jonathan Severdia, Sean Kelly, Julia Lillis, L. Kurschner, L. Day, Tom Farrell, Warren Z, Kris Gregorian, Brandon Murderous, Matthew & Candice Banta, Rich Thompson, Steve York, and Party Michelle. Woohoo! That's like 25 copies sold. If we forgot your name, and you want to get back at us, you should buy a copy of this book and we'll feel really bad for not including you. Really bad.

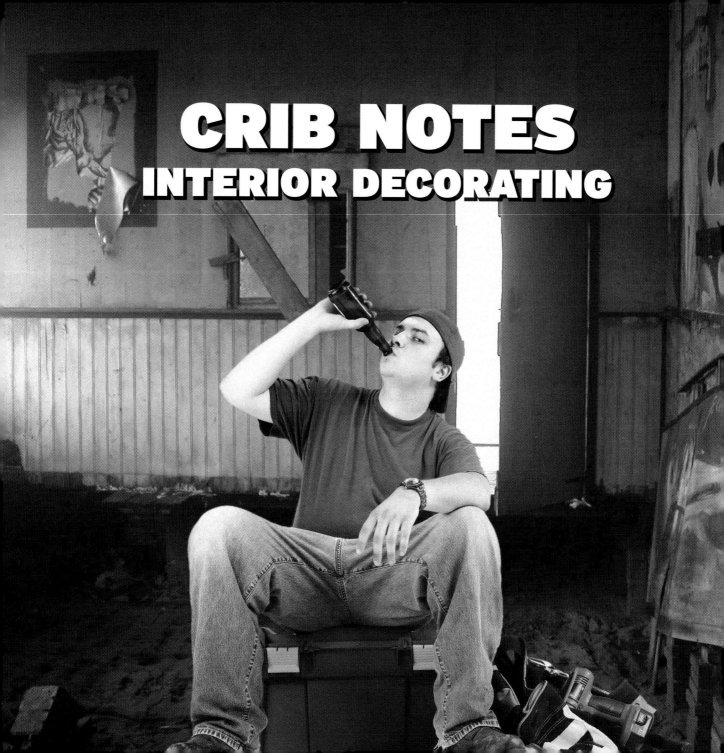

# CRIB NOTES
## INTERIOR DECORATING

# How to Build
# A Vibrating Couch or Bed
## . . . . World's Largest Sex Toy

Imagine a couch or bed that vibrated to whatever music you were listening to – vertebrae-cracking death metal, booty-shaking hip hop, or even tear-jerking emo.

The party applications of this device are freaking awesome.

- Mix drinks simply by sticking them between your legs.
- Have that dance party for deaf people you always wanted.
- Finally justify your horrible taste in techno music.

How do you improve an electric toothbrush? Make it vibrate. How do you improve a razor with ten blades? Make it vibrate. How do you improve a couch? Add a hot chick.

Look, there are some pieces of decor that you just can't buy at the store that'll make ladies swoon over your manliness: a mounted deer's head, a golden throne, and a vibrating couch.

How do you improve upon a soft comfortable couch?

Add some pillows, maybe an Afghan?

In the 1970's, people would spend up to 25 cents just to sit on a vibrating bed. Adjusted for inflation, that's the equivalent of $4 million today.

# Getting Started

**Cost:**
$100+

**Difficulty:**
You were technically-inclined as a child right?

**Time:**
About 2 hours (includes time to find stuff)

**Stuff You Need:**
- A bass shaker, aka butt shakers, or sonic transducers (see examples on next page)
- An amplifier (ideally one out of a powered subwoofer)
- Stereo speaker hook up wire
- An RCA Cable

WARNING:
This is one of the most boring How-To's of the book to READ, but it is one of the coolest inventions to DO. Just read the instructions in some boring math class and they will seem more entertaining.

# Selecting Your Booty Shakers or Amp

## Examples of Bass Shakers, Booty Shakers, or If You're Talking to the Old Guy at the Store: "Sonic Transducers"

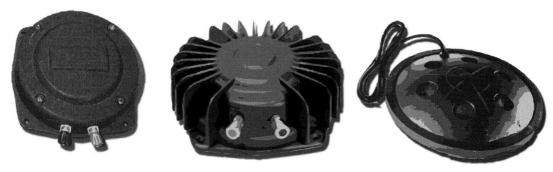

### The Amp:
An amp out of a powered subwoofer will work best because these amplifiers throw away all of the higher frequencies like vocals.

Running high frequencies into the bass shakers will cause them to emit funny sounds.

Although it can't be much worse than when Jeremy sings in the shower.

You will have a singing couch, and it can sound pretty bad, as these things are not designed to play back those sounds.

Alternatives:
If the subwoofer amp is not available, a standard stereo amp will do. Turn the treble controls all of the way down, and the bass controls all the way up, to minimize funny noises coming out of the bass shaker.

I have no idea what any of this means.

IN$IDE FINANCE:
Seat a bunch of friends on your vibrating couch, and you'll make a fortune in lost change.

## 1

### *If You Are Using a Standard Amplifier*

Hook the new amplifier as a slave to your existing stereo system using a record output on the existing (master) amplifier. This will make the slave amplifier receive the same music that is playing on the master system. See diagram.

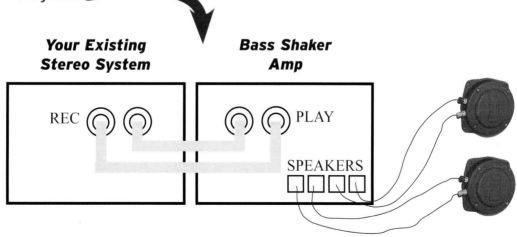

*Your Existing
Stereo System*

*Bass Shaker
Amp*

REC

PLAY

SPEAKERS

## 2 With an Amplifier Out of an Old Powered Subwoofer

Hook the "speaker out" to the "speaker in" from your existing system to the old sub amp.

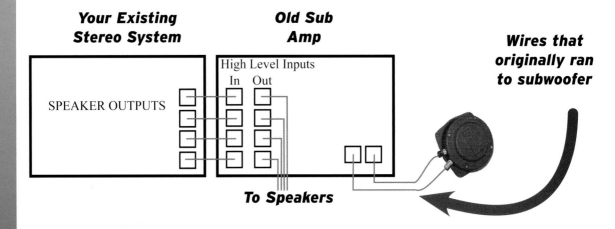

**Your Existing
Stereo System**

**Old Sub
Amp**

**Wires that
originally ran
to subwoofer**

SPEAKER OUTPUTS

High Level Inputs
In    Out

**To Speakers**

## 3 If You Are Using a Dolby Digital Amplifier

Hook the new amplifier to the LFE channel of the existing amplifier. For two bass shakers, an RCA Y cable will also be needed.

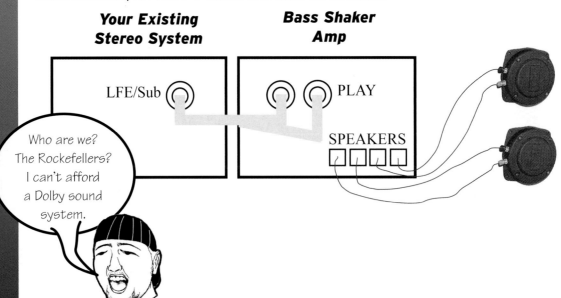

**Your Existing
Stereo System**

**Bass Shaker
Amp**

LFE/Sub

PLAY

SPEAKERS

Who are we?
The Rockefellers?
I can't afford
a Dolby sound
system.

### Pop That Ish Under a Cushion

A bass shaker placed under a couch cushion, or between the mattress and the box spring should produce a good vibration effect.

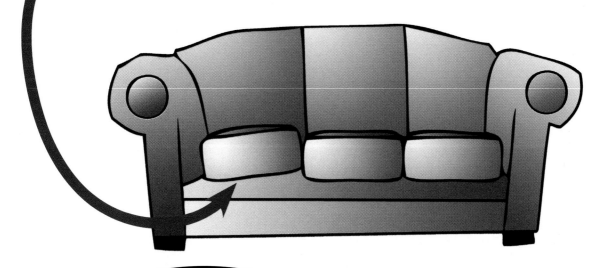

Tip: To increase the vibration effect, try mounting the bass shaker with screws underneath the frame of the couch, or the box spring of the bed.

**Nintendo Power Pro Player Tip:** Get on the couch with a female character. If you move up, down, up, down, right, left, up, up, up, up, up, up, up, up, up, you'll get her pregnant.

**Alternative to the Vibrating Couch....**
**You can just get really giant speakers.**

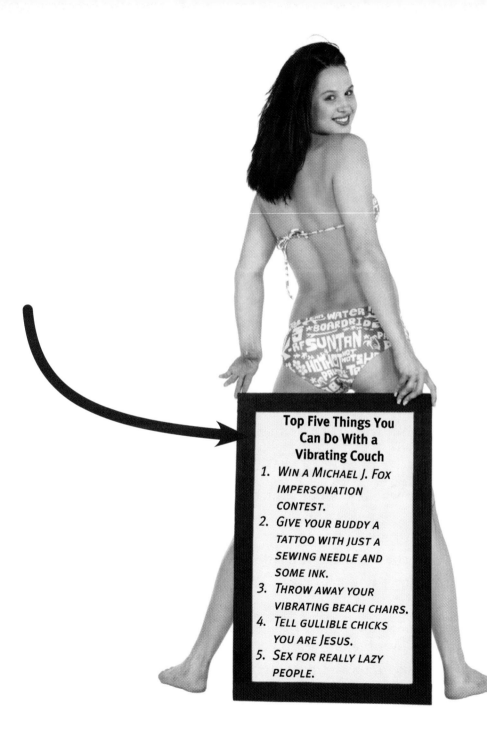

**Top Five Things You Can Do With a Vibrating Couch**

1. WIN A MICHAEL J. FOX IMPERSONATION CONTEST.
2. GIVE YOUR BUDDY A TATTOO WITH JUST A SEWING NEEDLE AND SOME INK.
3. THROW AWAY YOUR VIBRATING BEACH CHAIRS.
4. TELL GULLIBLE CHICKS YOU ARE JESUS.
5. SEX FOR REALLY LAZY PEOPLE.

# How to Build Furniture Out of Cardboard Boxes
## ... For Fine Hobo Living

Step aside Martha Stewart. Back of the line Ikea. An old refrigerator box is coming through and its earth tones will coordinate nicely with your Magnetic Wall (*page 38*) and Vibrating Couch (*page 2*) perfectly.

Unlike furniture from Ikea, the instructions are simple. No Allen wrenches or tiny screws or bolts. No directions in every language, but English. Just simple pictures that anyone with half a brain could follow.

Many people study the Oriental art of Feng Shui; others practice the craft of Origami, but who does both? You, now!

*I'm already confused!*

*I have a black belt in Origami.*

That's right, with a few folds of cardboard and some clear shipping tape you'll be able to make a jumping frog or a lotus flower... I mean a chair.

So run down to the corner and steal the home right out from over that homeless person. It will make you feel like a banker repossessing your house just to add a new piece of furniture to his mansion.

# Getting Started

**Voted the #1 Way to Impress Girls by Recycling**

**Cost:**
FREE

**Difficulty:**
C or better in Algebra and Geometry

**Time:**
About an hour

**Stuff You Need:**
- A Large Cardboard Moving Box
- Box Cutter
- Marking Pen
- Clear Shipping Tape

Ancient man built furniture out of rock. You're better than cave men, aren't you? That's right, you are. So use cardboard.

Cardboard is a fundamental building block in engineering.

Stop living that disgusting life, and start doing what the truly rich people, like Donald Trump and Oprah Winfrey do: make your own furniture. Oh, that's right; they DON'T build their own furniture, because they don't know how. And that's why they will forever remain losers. Unlike you, after you read and do the following.

Making a chair out of cardboard isn't very expensive, and it saves the rainforest.

So technically, ladies, I'm a hero.

In order to make things simple, the design is based upon squares. The scale is not given, but notice that the square that says SEAT is where you place your behind. So you should probably make that at least a foot-and-a-half wide.

Each cut out is comprised of five squares. If you are using the foot and a half scale, then the bottom should be three feet wide and three feet high on one side, four and half feet high on the other side. See Figure 1.

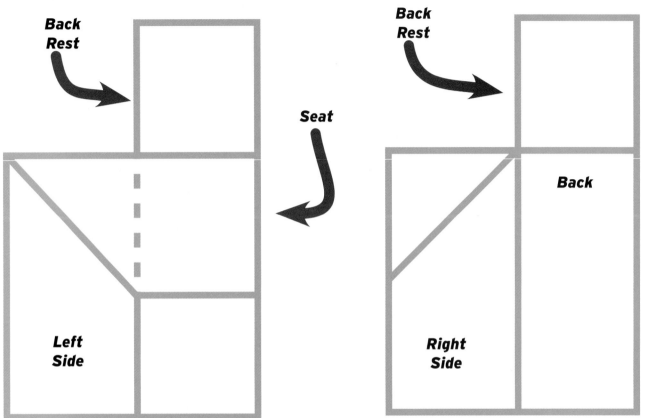

**Figure 1**

The solid lines are where you will be folding the cardboard.
Cut on the dotted line.

**IN$IDE FINANCE:**
With today's housing
market, more people will be
living in cardboard than ever before

You can use the edge of a cardboard piece to draw straight lines. Once you've drawn the designs of Figure 1 onto your cardboard and cut them out, fold according to the diagrams.

With furniture, you won't have to lean against the TV to have sex anymore.

After folding, you should have two complete halves of a chair. Fasten them together with clear shipping tape.

Your chair should look like this now.

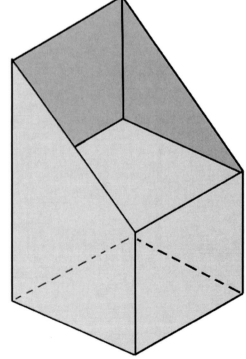

**Architectural Corner:**
For aesthetic purposes, renowned architect Frank Lloyd Wright insisted upon being buried in a cardboard box.

It may look like a chair, but don't sit in it just yet. Your chair needs to be reinforced.

2 Cut out two more pieces of cardboard. Like these:

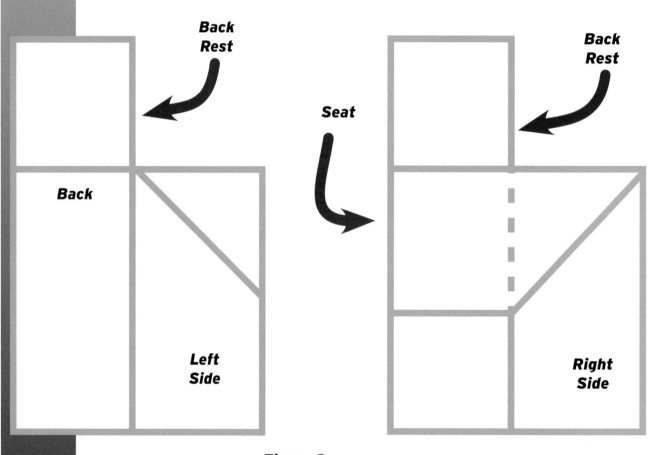

**Figure 2**

**3**

Fold according to the diagram and cut that dotted line. Place these reinforcement pieces over the chair, so they wrap around it, adding strength.

Tape down any loose pieces of cardboard, and generously apply tape to all seams.

Don't let anyone sit on your cardboard creations, if they set off the Fatty Detector (See page 210.)

**WARNING**
**Too many drinks spilled on your new chair may cause it to buckle.**

**TIP**

***Got Pets?***
Use a cereal box to make a mini-cardboard chair for your pet rat, hamster, or neighborhood midget.

On the following page, both of the diagrams are given again. Make a photocopy and cut out the figures to better understand how the chair will be assembled.

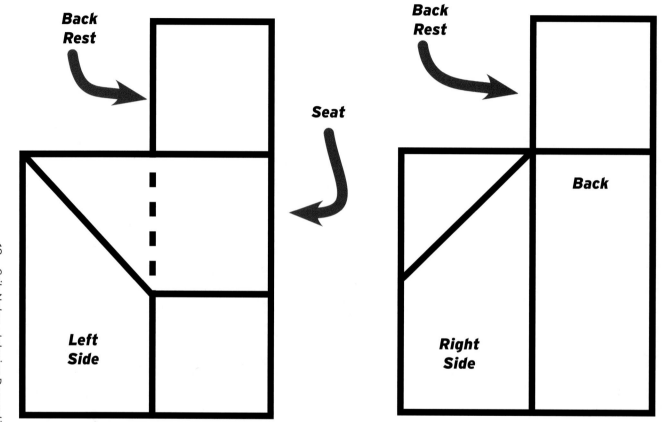

**Figure 1**

The solid black lines are where you will be folding the cardboard.
Cut on the dotted line.

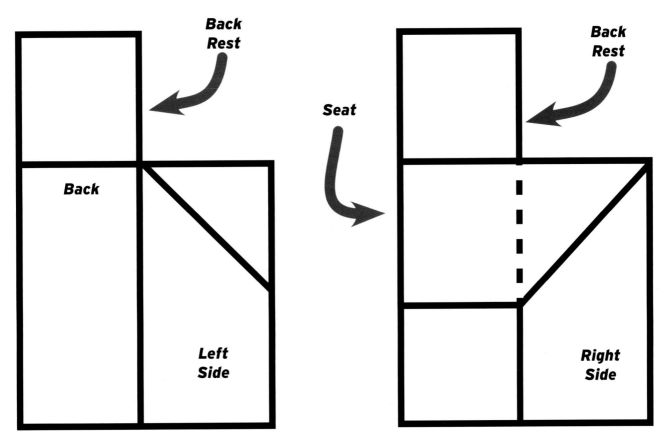

**Back Rest**

**Seat**

**Back Rest**

**Back**

**Left Side**

**Right Side**

**Figure 2**

# How to Build
# A 40-Ounce Lava Lamp
## . . . Because You're That Classy

For centuries on end, God tried to invent the lava lamp, but the closest He ever came was throwing lightning behind some clouds.

Lava lamps have been voted "Number One Most Trippy Thing to Look at When Wasted" time and time again. In fact, this has been proven conclusively by stoned scientists.

*I drank mine, and now my urine glows in the dark!*

This will provide hours of fun...well, not on its own, naturally, you'll probably need to add beer. But making your own out of a 40-oz bottle will impress anyone you have at your home, from foreign dignitaries to homeless prostitutes. When the S.W.A.T. team crashes through your windows, they'll see the 40-oz lava lamp and be all "super snap!" before unloading on you with dozens of tear gas bullets.

Building a lava lamp is actually pretty complicated – in fact, I wouldn't advise starting the project unless you're procrastinating for a really big final exam or serving 5 to 10 in prison. We know the chemicals used in a commercial lava lamp, but the chemicals in it aren't toxic enough for us. Follow these directions and you may uncover the secret, but you also might end up with a puddle of muddy goop, a broken bottle, and a shattered dream.

# Getting Started

**Cost:**
$50

**Difficulty:**
Depends upon whether you found a 40-oz bottle that was full or empty.

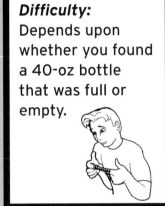

**Time:**
Like a billion years. If you start and finish this project, send us photos.

**Stuff You Need:**
- 1 Empty 40 oz. malt liquor bottle (preferably clear). Any bottle will do, but narrow/tall bottles work better than short/fat bottles.
- 90% Isopropyl Alcohol (Rubbing Alcohol from the drug store)
- 1 Bottle Mineral Oil (again from a drug store) or Motor Oil. Using motor oil will leave you with no color choices.
- 1 40 Watt bulb and fixture.
- 2 Large Soup Cans (32 ounces) or other base.
- 1 Plug in Lamp, dimmer (optional).
- Food coloring (optional)
- Electrical Tape
- Kosher Salt (optional)

**Before Starting, Think Long and Hard About Your Life Goals:**
This is one of the hardest projects in this book. And when you take into account that commercial lava lamps are only $30, the only real reason to attempt to make your own is either

    A.  You like a challenge or

    B.  You are trapped in the lair of an evil madman bent on world domination and the only way to escape is to build a lava lamp out of a 40-ounce.

**1**

But if you're actually going to try and make this thing:

First, find an old broken lamp.

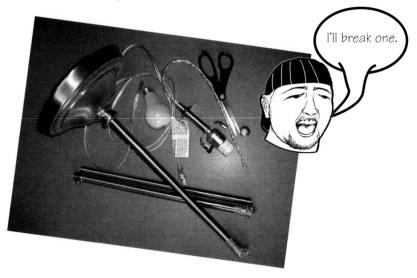

I'll break one.

**2**

Remove everything so that you're left with a socket and a cord. (You may have to cut the cord to get it out of the old lamp.) Construct a stand so that the socket will stand straight up. We used electrical tape and some leftover pieces from the lamp.

**3** Next, construct a base for the 40 watt bulb out of the soup can.  The light bulb will be in this housing and the bottle will rest on top of the can.

**4** Empty two 32 ounce cans. Remove both lids from one can, but leave one lid on the other, and cut a hole in the top of that can.
Poke another hole for the lamp cord on the side of the can, but remove any sharp edges by filing them down, so the cord doesn't fray.

## ECO-TIP
Recycling a forty-ounce bottle will get you a quarter.
A lamp costs $20.
Recycling is useless.

# 5

Run the cord through the can and reconnect the wires using electrical tape. Place the bulb and stand in the housing unit. Plug it in and make sure it works.

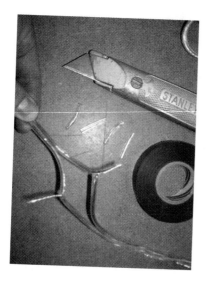

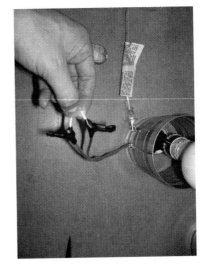

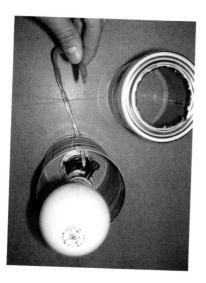

# 6

Wrap the two cans together with electrical tape.

# 7

Remove the label from the 40, if you want, by soaking it in hot water. Fill the 40-oz. bottle most of the way up with the rubbing alcohol. Add 2-4 ounces of mineral oil.

This mineral oil will be the lava, so add an appropriate amount for flow.

Even if you love lava, keep it to about 5%-10% of the total. The bottle should now be most of the way full.

Place the mostly full bottle on top of the 40 watt bulb fixture and base.

The bottle should be 1 to 2 inches above the bulb, no farther, and definitely not touching the bulb.

Adding Color:

If color is desired, both the water, and the oil (the lava) can be dyed before mixing.

Remember that water soluble dyes will affect the water, and that oil soluble dyes will dye the mineral oil (the lava).

- Food coloring, and children's paints are both water soluble.
- Oil based dyes can be obtained easily by cutting apart a permanent marker.

**8** Turn on the bulb, and leave on about an hour for it to come up to the proper temperature. After the bottle is up to temperature, fill a turkey baster or something similar with water.

A dimmer switch can help fine tune the lamp for optimum performance by allowing the amount of heat to be controlled. Too much lava action, turn down the dimmer.

**9** Add water to the mixture very slowly (a few drops a minute), until the oil starts to lift.

Don't add the water too fast: it needs to mix throughout the rubbing alcohol before any effect will be observed.

A chopstick can be used to lightly stir the mixture, which may speed the process up somewhat.

**10** When the oil starts to ball and rise, you have the correct mixture. Cap the bottle, and let it run for a while.

If the oil stays at the top of the bottle you have added too much. Adjust with more rubbing alcohol, or a very small pinch of kosher salt, until the oil sinks slightly.

 **WARNING**

**I can't repeat it enough:**
This project can be motherfucking dangerous.
Dirty Mike almost burned down the house - twice.
You may want to have the Fire Marshall nearby or 911 on speed dial.

# How to Make
# A Duct Tape Wallet
## . . . To Hold Your Monopoly Money

Tired of having your wallet stolen for its precious leather? The next time you're held up at gunpoint, flash a duct tape wallet and the thief will give up on your apparently broke ass. Either that or he'll be so pissed you wasted his time that he shoots you, but that's the risk you take for stylin'.

Okay, so that hypothetical may not have enticed you into building a wallet out of duct tape, but believe me, there are many more hypothetical situations where that one came from.

- Did your grandma give you a roll of duct tape for Christmas instead of that cool wallet you were asking for?
  *Then this "How-to" is for you!*

- Does the girl you like have a duct-tape fetish?
  *Then this "How-to" is for you!*

- Are you entering a contest for duct tape crafters, but don't really want to win or get noticed at all?
  *Then this "How-to" is for you!*

There are over infinity reasons to make a wallet out of duct tape!

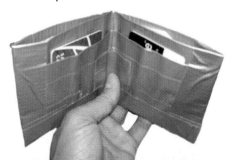

That's right; we own stock in Duct Tape Corporation.

# Getting Started

**Cost:**
Under $10

**Difficulty:**
Duct tape can be
very frustrating to
work with.

**Time:**
Half an hour.
Unless you're not
good with sticky
objects.

**Stuff You Need:**
- 1 Roll Duct Tape
- Ruler
- Razor Blade or Exacto Knife or Box Cutter or Ninja Sword
- 2 Steady Hands or 1 Box of Bandaids

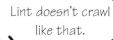

It's taking the lint out of my hair.

Lint doesn't crawl like that.

Anything that you can make out of leather you can also make out of duct tape, by creating sheets of overlapping adhered duct tape strips. For short, we'll call these pieces of material "duct leather."

Duck leather? That makes about as much sense as cow feathers or buffalo wings.

Start by overlapping strips of duct tape. For the wallet, you should use strips about 9 inches long. Lay the smooth side down. Then place another 9 inch strip over the top half of the piece that's laid down, sticky side on sticky side.

## 2

Repeat this process by covering the bottom half with another 9 inch strip – sticky side to sticky side, of course. Flip this over and repeat. See how you are making a sheet of sturdy and smooth "duct leather?"

You'll need about ten strips to make the wallet. There will be an extra half a strip sticky side on the top and bottom. Before you fold them over, make sure that the dimensions will be at least 7 by 8 inches.

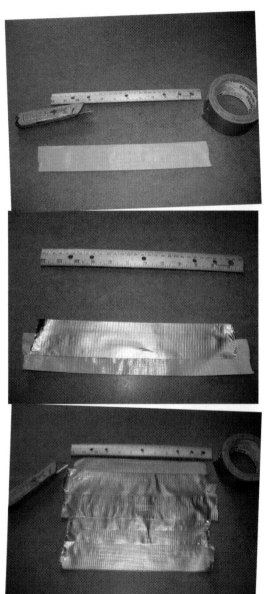

With your razor blade or Exacto knife or box cutter or ninja sword, cut a rectangle 7" x 8". This will be the main casing of the wallet.

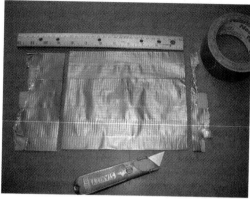

Fold it in half and duct tape the two small sides together. You see it? It's a wallet!

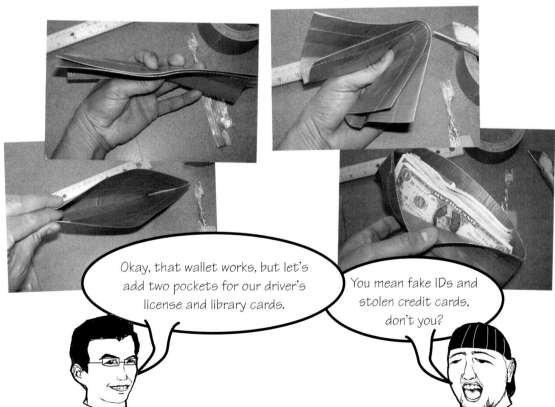

Okay, that wallet works, but let's add two pockets for our driver's license and library cards.

You mean fake IDs and stolen credit cards, don't you?

# Adding Credit Card and ID Sleeves

**4** Using the same process as before, create a piece of duct leather and cut out a 3" x 8" rectangle.

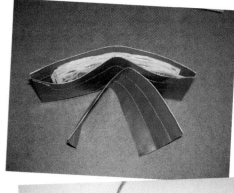

*Money saved by not buying a wallet*

Lay this on top of your wallet. Notice how it has the same width but it's not as tall.

Place a piece of cardboard into your wallet where your money would go.

**5** With your razor blade, cut a one inch slit down the center of this new piece and also through the inside layer of your wallet. DO NOT CUT all the way through to the outside of the wallet.

## TRICKY PART

**6** Cut a half-inch long piece of duct tape. Run it through the slit half way and then adhere the extra flap to the wallet. Run another half-inch strip of duct tape through the slit the other way and adhere.
Repeat two or three more times so that the extra flap is tightly secured to the wallet through the flap.

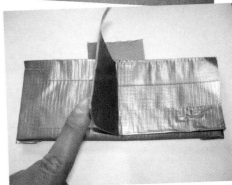

# 7

Last step, seal the side and bottom edges together with duct tape. Double tape corners for extra strength.

That's it. Insert a couple Ben Franklins and hit the town.

> Will it hold George Washingtons? Can I make a duct tape coin purse?

**Xmas Savings!**
According to Jeremy's calculations, you can make up to 40 wallets with a single roll of duct tape.

> That's 38 more than my Christmas list!

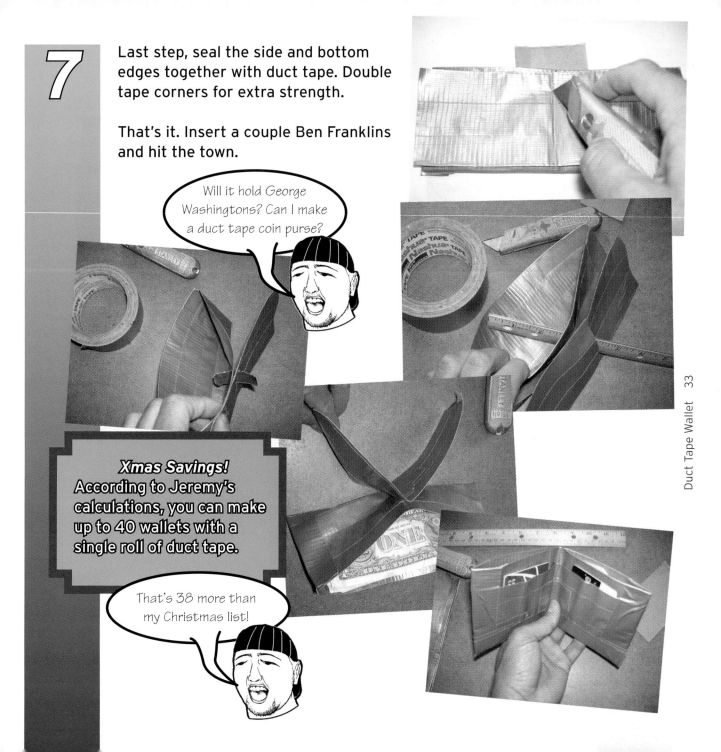

# More Duct Tape Projects

Anything that we can make out of leather we can also make out of duct tape.

## How to Make a Belt Out of Duct Tape

**1**

First take a look at one of your own belts. Pretty basic, eh? It's just a long strip of leather with holes on one side and a buckle on the other side.

To get started, pull out long strips of duct tape and carefully construct a long piece of "duct leather." The length of your belt should equal your waist size, plus 8 inches.

**2**

Working with strips of duct tape this long can be a real pain. You should probably have a friend nearby to help out and hold the sticky tape.

Rolls of duct tape are usually 1.75 inches wide, and most belts are between 1 and 1.5 inches wide. Cut yours to the desired width.

Jeremy! Help!

**3**

Cut the corners off the end of your belt. This is going to be the most difficult part of your belt to deal with. Some people choose to cut the corners last.

Two layers of duct tape would make for a really flimsy belt; add layers of duct tape to make this a belt that will last forever.

**4**

Wrap duct tape around your belt in the opposite direction, and then wrap tape around your belt diagonally. This will increase its strength and make it thicker. Do this on both sides of the belt.

Once your belt is nice and thick, you may want to put long strips of duct tape running the length of the belt. Remember, working with a piece of tape that long is a pain. Make sure to have a buddy help you out.

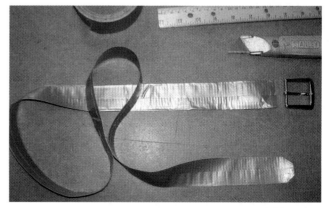

Now we have a long strip of belt without any holes, or a buckle, or a belt loop.

**5** With your ruler, mark off where to drill 4 to 5 small holes.
Important note: The first hole closest to the end of the belt needs to be about 4 inches up. Space the holes about .8 inches apart.

**6** Now let's build the belt loop. Make a piece of duct leather about one half inch thick and one half inch longer than twice the width of your belt. Make sure to make your belt loop about the same thickness as the belt.

**7** Fold two inches of the top of the belt down over the buckle. Cut a sliver into the belt so that the metal prong can poke through. Then wrap the belt over the inside bar of the buckle.

**8** Line up the belt loop with the flap holding the buckle into place. Tape everything down and reinforce.

You now have a duct tape wallet and matching belt. What else could you make to let the world know that you're crafty?

# How to Make a Duct Tape Tie

Go into your dad's closet and grab one of his expensive silk ties. You know, they're right next to the Playboys he thinks are hidden.

That tie is your pattern. Create a piece of duct leather a slightly bigger than the tie, lay the tie on top, trace it out, then cut out with a razor blade. Voila!

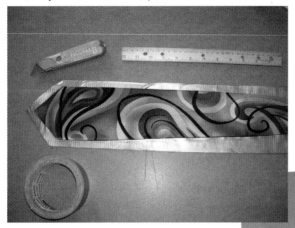

> If it acts like a duck and quacks like a duck, then I can make anything out of it.

We suggest you don't wear your duct tape tie to any interviews unless, of course, you're trying to get a job at Home Depot.

# How to Build
# A Magnetic Poster Wall
## . . . 'Cuz Your Music Taste Changes Every Five Seconds

I can see why that lady became a carpenter. She's flat as a board!

These days, keeping up with music is a full-time job. You have tens of band friend requests every day on MySpace alone. If you aren't in a band yourself, then your roommate is. Everywhere you turn there is a new "musician" with a nose ring (are those still in?) for you to fall in love with, but you still have that stale-ass Green Day poster on the wall!

Get with the times! You should be changing posters on your wall five times a day – or at least between meals.

Ironically, my favorite band is called "The Magnetic Walls."

The magnetic wall is also a great way to put up notes for yourself, photos, or whatever else you need to hang up. Best thing is, when the girl of your dreams comes over, the one who loves My Chemical Romance, you can slap a poster up on the wall and make her swoon. You can tell her that you're the bassist if you paste a picture of your face over one of the dudes in the band.

What are you waiting for? Just reading this page put you about 20 music-styles behind so go get your magnetation on!

# Getting Started

**S
W
E
E
T**

**Cost:**
Around $40
bucks

**Difficulty:**
Some high school
required (more
than you need
to get into 9th
grade, but less
than you need for
college)

**Time:**
About two
hours (or 40
new pop song
cycles)

**Stuff You Need:**
- Paint Roller
- Two-Inch Wide Paint Brush
- Roll of Painter's Tape
- At Least 2 Quarts of Magnetic Paint
- Small, thin magnets
- Poster of your roommate's shitty band

This might be the longest and least fun of all the projects, but it's one of the coolest. In a nutshell, all you are doing is painting.

But here's the twist: you'll need Magnetic Paint, sometimes called magnetic primer. It should be stocked at your local hardware store: if you can't find it on your own, ask for assistance.

If you live in the boondocks, you can order magnetic paint online. But paint is heavy, so shipping costs may make an expensive project even more costly.

Labor is free, if you go into Tom Sawyer mode and round up a bunch of friends and sucker them in by telling them how much fun it is to paint a wall.

Okay, so you'll probably be doing this project alone. No worries. Here's what you need to know: paint makes a mess. Use tape to mark the edges and lay down tarps or several layers of newspaper.

Also, magnetic paint needs to be applied in many coats. On the can, the manufacturer will recommend about four coats. Four coats! That's a whole day of painting and waiting around.

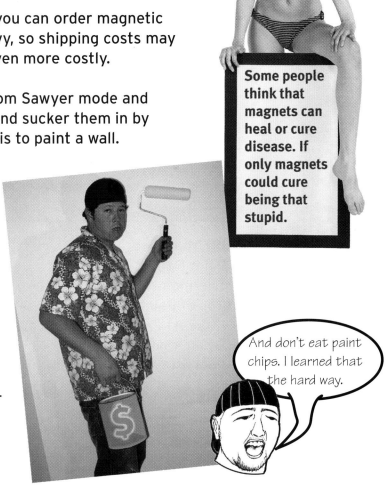

Some people think that magnets can heal or cure disease. If only magnets could cure being that stupid.

And don't eat paint chips. I learned that the hard way.

Besides a lot of time, another downside of this project is price. Magnetic paint costs about $20 per quart. To paint four coats on a section of wall about ten feet wide and eight feet high will take two quarts.

In other words, to paint your whole living room, will take about two days and cost about $200. Oh, and we still need to buy magnets!

But I recommend at least SIX coats!!! Magnetic paint isn't very strong.

Why would you want to do more than one magnetic wall?

I have a magnetic Spiderman outfit. So we're painting the ceiling too.

So you've got a magnetic wall.... Now what should you do with it?

I know!

## *How to Make a Giant Poster of Your Face:*
## *Or Something Less Egotistical*

Now that you have a Magnetic Poster Wall, you need something to hang on it. It's obvious: you're the most famous person on the planet. Everywhere you go, you hear your name dropped. But, it's not fair that only people who are near you can see your face. It's almost cruel even.

By now, you should be totally convinced that this is the best project ever. Consider this argument - it's a giant picture of your face! If you don't think that a giant picture of your face is the greatest thing ever, then buddy you need to wrap your arm in self esteem and take a big old needle full of American Pride straight to the vein!

Ever feel used when people come over to your place for a party? They're just there for the liquor. They probably don't even know whose house it is. Well, not anymore! Your 10-foot giant head glaring at them from above the keg will send the message loud and clear "Y'all betta recognize!"

The only remaining thought in your head now should be "How do I get my face to as many needy people as possible?" That's an easy question: hot air balloon.

# Getting Started

**Cost:**
$0

**Difficulty:**
None

**Time:**
About twenty minutes

**Stuff You Need:**
- The Internet
- A printer

**1** Go to this web site: http://homokaasu.org/rasterbator/

**2** Print.

**3** Put the result up on your wall.

Finally, a project for me!

If the Rasterbator doesn't exist by the time this book comes out...

Go to Kinko's.

*If you had a tiny poster of your face, it would be called a "stamp."*

Did You Know

DID YOU KNOW...
Colonel Sanders has a
300-foot-wide billboard of
himself in Nevada.
This move got him
a lot of bedroom
play.

**Top 5 Most Common Causes of Death for Glam Rockers:**
1. Toxic Face-Glitter Syndrome
2. Drowning after falling asleep in a giant hair grease puddle.
3. Crushed in threesome with fat groupies.
4. Putting lead-based mascara on your tongue
5. Old-age

**BTW**

### Magnets, Schmagnets
You'll need like a billion magnets to hold up all the pieces of paper for this project...so you might just want to use tape.
Sorry about that whole magnetic wall thing.

> Or buy a billion magnets. I own stock in Magnet Co., too.

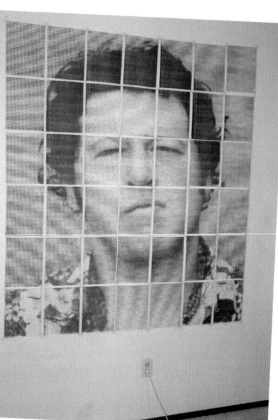

# How to Build
# An Invisible Book Shelf
## . . . Since Reading is Magical

*As if the library wasn't creepy enough*

The fact that you're reading this sentence tells us that you know how to read, and may own some books. Where do you keep them? Some crappy bookshelf, where they only fill half a shelf, tipping over, and knocking down your bong? That's ridiculous! Any Feng Shui expert would say that your books should be floating in midair to maximize your alliance with the Universe.

*I have a black belt in Feng Shui.*

Design is important, when you show people around your apartment you want them to say, "Wow, that's kinda cool, I guess." Nothing does this more resoundingly than a bunch of books clinging on the wall, as if by magic.

*Hypothetically, is an invisible bookshelf a good place to hide stolen goods?*

**FYI** In the 17th century, this invention could have gotten you burned for witchcraft.

# Getting Started

**Cost:**
$20 + the cost of whatever textbooks you're never going to read

**Difficulty:**
+3 Wizardry
(Sorry, Neville)

**Time:**
1 hour +
1 night to dry

**Stuff You Need:**
- 2 Large "L" Brackets
- Box Cutter
- 10 One-Inch Long Drywall Screws
- Level
- Wood Glue
- At least one book

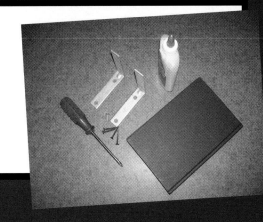

**1**

There's nothing really too magical about the Invisible Book Shelf. We're merely going to hide our "L" brackets inside of a book.

Sorry, Sci-Fi nerds.

Most shelves rest on top of the "L" brackets. But you're going to use your "L" bracket to hold up your shelf that is made out of a book.

**2**

First, you'll need to decide how large you'd like your bookshelf to be. Then find a book of that size you don't mind sacrificing.
Say, Bill Maher's latest tome, *New Rules*.

New Rule:
You can't publish transcripts of your television show and try to sell it as a book.

I don't have any books. Oh wait, how about THIS book?

No, that's a magazine. Find a book that's bigger and has a hard cover.

**3**

Using the edge of a work bench, open the back cover of the book. Evenly space the two "L" brackets and then secure the brackets into the book with the 1 inch dry wall screws. So make sure that your book is thicker than 1 inch.

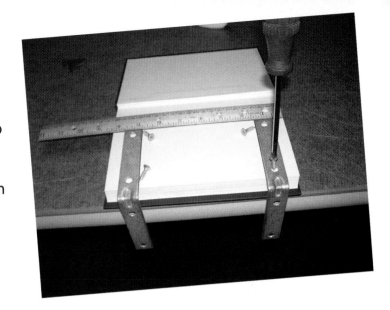

**4**

The "L" brackets should be hanging over the edge of your work table. But if you were to drill this into the wall right now, the back flap would dangle.

That's where the glue comes in.

"Flap Dangle" would be a good pornstar name.

**5** Apply a lot of glue to the back cover and shut it on top of the brackets. Then place something heavy on top of the book and let the glue dry for at least 8 hours.

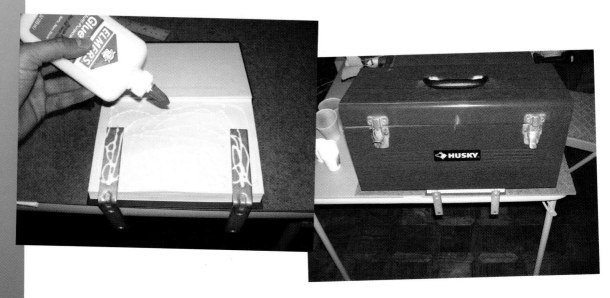

**6** Once the glue is dry, find a cool place to hang your Invisible Book Shelf.

**7** Also, make sure you use a level when you hang your "book" shelf.

There's nothing worse than a crooked book magically floating on your wall.

**8** Although you can still see where the "L" brackets are screwed into the wall above this book, once you've stacked a few more books on top your "book" shelf, voila, it looks as though that stack of books are magically floating on the wall.

If you want to go the extra mile, you can paint over the bracket to match your wall.

**9** Say the magic word "Shazaaaaam!"

Questions for Discussion:

1. What would pioneer settlers have thought if the Indians had presented them with an invisible bookshelf at the first Thanksgiving? Would they have shot the Native Americans that much faster? Explain your answer loudly on the street corner of a reservation.

2. If you had invented the invisible bookshelf during the Middle Ages, would the bubonic plague still have killed as many hot women? Why, or why not?

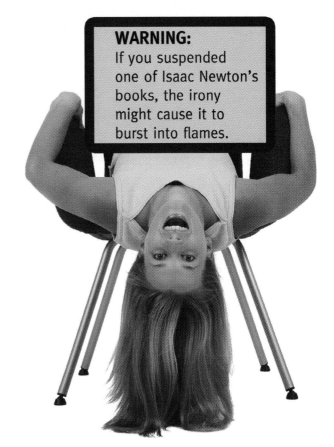

**WARNING:**
If you suspended one of Isaac Newton's books, the irony might cause it to burst into flames.

*Alphabet Crypt-O-Gram:*
*When your friends see this,*
*they will say:*
*XNNNNNNNNX!*

(answer: WOOOOOOOOOM!)

# How to Build
# A Beer Bottle Oil Lamp
## . . . Not a Molotov Cocktail

Every party should have a room set up for the ladies. Somewhere they can feel relaxed, and maybe even make out with you. But since you don't have a bunch of stuffed unicorns and frilly drapes on hand, mood lighting is the only way to make that pig sty look remotely attractive.

Fortunately, our experts have devised a way to make seductive oil lamps, using stuff you probably have lying around your bathroom floor, like beer bottles. A couple of these lamps will turn any ugly room into a hard-to-see Den of Passion™.

So what are you waiting for? You too can light your home or backyard party just like they did in olden times. Back then there were wenches, maidens, and dragons and shit. And then Thomas Edison had to go and invent the light bulb. What a buzz killer.

Just like a strip club!

Oil lamps burn brighter than candles. If only we could invent a type of fire lamp that you could knock over without burning down the house.

# Getting Started

**Cost:**
Around five bucks each

**Difficulty:**
This would be a kindergarten project if it didn't involve fire.

**Time:**
20 minutes

**Stuff You Need:**
- 32oz or 40oz bottle (with metallic screw on lid)
- Bottle of Cooking Oil (preferably Olive Oil) or Lamp Oil
- Funnel
- Cotton sock (or cotton rope clothesline)
- Thick nail
- Hammer
- Scissors
- Food Coloring

Any bottle will work, but a clear glass bottle with a twist off top, works best. A forty ounce of Old E can set the mood for a romantic, yet still gangsta', evening.

**1**

Place the cap flat side down, on a working surface, perhaps a phonebook. Hammer a nail through the top. Wiggle the nail around and remove it. You want this hole to be big enough so that the cotton rope or sock wick can barely be pulled through.

**2**

An old Phillips screwdriver used after the nail may make the hole big enough.

Make sure it's an old screwdriver, because this isn't good for a screwdriver.

**3**

To make a sock wick: cut the top of the sock off, especially if the sock has elastic on the top half. Then cut up and down the sock, spirally, for a wick as long as the bottle.

**WARNING**

Only a 100% cotton sock should be used as a wick. Plastic or synthetic fabric will burn too fast and give off toxic fumes. If you don't have a cotton sock, you can cut a sliver of cloth wick from any other pure cotton material, such as a T-shirt, or buy cotton clothesline.

I used an old pair of tighty-whities.

**4** Run the rope or wick through the hole in the cap, leaving a quarter inch of wick sticking out through the top.

**NOTE**

Your workspace for the rest of this project, should be somewhere that won't burst into flames if you spill the oil. In other words, make this outdoors!

**5**

With a funnel, fill the bottle with lamp oil or a cooking oil which will smell good when burned (we recommend extra virgin olive oil.)

However, lamp oil burns better than cooking oil, whose flame can be extinguished outdoors by a light breeze.

But whichever oil you choose, thread the wick or cotton wick through the cap, down into the oil, screw the cap on, light the wick, and you've got yourself a somewhat romantic oil lamp!

Extra virgin? Is that even possible?

But what if you want to get a little more romantic and fancy? You know that oil floats on water, right?

It also sticks to seagulls, and seals and penguins.

Before you pour the oil, fill your bottle halfway up with water, and add some food color to dye the water if you're feeling really crazy.

When it's placed in the bottle, the wick shouldn't touch the water level - line up the wick with the bottle, eye the length, and cut any excess rope or wick before insertion.

*If Bob Seger were alive, today, he'd say, "Dude, you doofus. I'm totally still alive."*

# 7

Gently pour the oil on top of the water. See how it floats? Then screw the cap with the wick back onto the bottle.

Did you say screw? Hahaha.

This is a How-To book. We're going to say "screw" a lot.

Ahem, twist the cap back on, and there you go: a homemade Tiki Table Torch.

**Personal Testimony:**
Steven Stevenson, 21, Nebraska
"I made this oil lamp, and the next week I got laid. That's a 100% magic invention."

# How to Build
# A Love Hammock
## . . . Must Supply Your Own Partner

Pretend you're lucky enough to pick up a woman in, let's say, your backyard. But in the time it would take you two to walk into the house and up to your bedroom, she could lose interest in you.

Not a chance. I always wear Axe.

Well what if you forgot that day?

You mean like how I forget to brush my teeth every morning?

**Love hammocks were first used by cavemen to trap sexual partners.**

Which is why we've developed the two-person love hammock. Not only can you enjoy hours of eye-hemorrhaging, swinging sex in your hammock, you'll have the perfect place to pass out afterward, without risking injury from rubber-knee walking.

Our test subjects reported a variety of benefits while using our love hammock: including increased vigor, stamina, and donkey-punch rebound. No wonder Anna Nicole Smith wanted to live out her final days in a love hammock.

# Getting Started

**Cost:**
Under $20

**Difficulty:**
It's about as tough as level 3-1 on Super Mario Brothers.

**Time:**
15 minutes

**Stuff You Need:**
- King Size Sheet
- 10 Feet of Rope
- 2 Palm Trees and a Tropical Beach

You'll be surprised at how simple it is to make a hammock. The only difficulty may be finding two things sturdy enough to hang it between.

Trees are ideal, of course, but what if you want to relax and "hang out" in your living room or dorm room? That's when you'll need to get creative; like running a rope through your upstairs neighbor's window or drilling giant eye screws into the studs in a wall.

**WARNING: DO NOT HANG YOUR LOVE HAMMOCK FROM YOUR LOVE POLE.**

But let's assume that you already have two sturdy things to tie your hammock between.

**1** Let's build that hammock! Mash a king-sized sheet lengthwise so that it's a thick bunched-up mess, and tie a simple knot at each end.

**2** Then depending on the distance between the two supports and length of the hammock, cut your rope sections to size. (It's better to have a few feet of extra of rope at each end, than not enough.) Tie a loose knot at one end of each rope section, and slip each of these knots over each end of the sheet directly below the large knot of bunched material you tied earlier.

Any basic knot will work to hold your hammock up, but we recommend a slip knot.

**3** Tighten both rope knots and make sure they're secure.  Then fasten each rope to a palm tree (or the giant eye screws drilled into your wall studs.)

Note:   Eye screws must be attached to a vertical stud behind the wall. (If you don't know how to find a stud, ask your mom about the guy she was dating before your dad.) Also, once your hammock is up, test it to make sure it will hold your weight (and another 100 pounds, or more, of girl) and that your knots are strong enough.

This guy is going to make love to himself in the woods. Way to go Love Hammock!

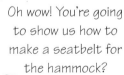

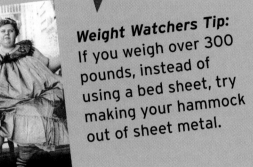

**Weight Watchers Tip:**
If you weigh over 300 pounds, instead of using a bed sheet, try making your hammock out of sheet metal.

If you break your hammock, don't bother rebuilding until you have raised your standards.

## How to Build a Hammock Chair

Hammocks are great for lying down, but if you want to sit up then you need a hammock chair.

I want to put a hammock chair in my car.

That wouldn't be very safe. You need to wear a seatbelt.

Oh wow! You're going to show us how to make a seatbelt for the hammock?

The Hammock Chair is actually easier to construct than the love hammock, since it doesn't need two supports: you can hang our hammock from a strong beam.

**1** Making the hammock chair starts off just like a regular hammock. Mash your king-sized sheet lengthwise so that it's a thick bunched up mess, but you only need to tie in a knot at one end, which will be the top of the chair hammock.

**2** Then, open up the bottom of the sheet and tie large knots in both of the two corners. These will be your two arm rests. (See the picture on the next page.)

**3** You'll need three lengths of rope to hang the hammock chair. Again, attach the rope slip knots below the knots in the sheet. Adjust the lengths to customize your hanging chair.

But since your hammock chair (and you) will be hanging from only one point, an eye screw alone won't be enough support.

It is much safer to hang your hammock chair from a beam.

# FIGHTING STARVATION

## COOKING

# How to
# Cook Without Pots and Pans
## . . . The Perfect Grilled Cheese

You can learn a lot in your freshmen year of college: how to download mp3s, talk a girl into doing your laundry, and cook in your dorm room with the bare essentials.

But if you skipped Dorm Cuisine 101 and are wondering how to cook without a stove or an oven, we're here to tell you: it's easy! All you need is a source of heat: you know, something that gets hot.

Look around; you've got light bulbs, a coffee maker, and maybe even a curling iron. Wait a second, where the heck did that curling iron come from?

Sure, you could break into the neighborhood market at 2 a.m. for a food raid, but the cops sounded kinda serious when they threatened you with jail time the last time you did that.

Anyhow, girls dig a guy that can cook. Especially a guy that can make them a grilled cheese sandwich on his iron at two in the morning.
Yeah! Kiss the chef.

Chicks say that I'm pretty hot.

It wasn't a threat. I was in jail for 3 days.

# Getting Started

**Cost:**
Around $2 bucks

**Difficulty:**
Piece of cake... wouldn't that be delicious right now?

**Time:**
About five minutes

Cooking on an iron can be dangerous. Make sure that you're of sound and sober mind when taking on this task.
Don't fall asleep with the iron on! And make extra sure you don't fall asleep on the iron!

**Stuff You Need:**
- Iron
- Tin Foil
- Bread
- Sliced Cheese
- Butter

Cooking grilled cheese on an iron? If people find out about this I'll lose millions!!

Don't tell George, but you can also use an iron to heat up week-old pizza.

**1** Butter two pieces of bread and throw some cheese in between.

Cooking without pans can be fun and flavorful. This is the type of ingenuity that will impress your utensil-dependent friends.

**2** Wrap the entire sandwich in foil. If you can afford it, double wrap it.

I went to Tijuana once and had to double wrap it.

Place another piece of tin foil on your ironing board. (If you don't have an ironing board, any nonflammable flat surface will work.)
Place the wrapped sandwich on the foil covered-surface. Turn your iron on High and place it on top of the sandwich.

Flip the foil-covered sandwich every couple minutes. If you have oven mitts (or hockey mitts) you can take a peak inside the foil to see if the sandwich is toasted to your liking.

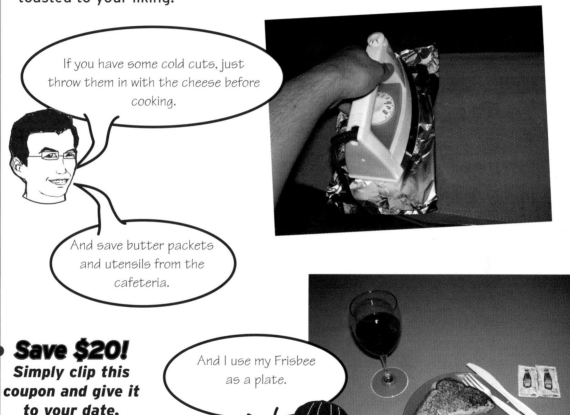

If you have some cold cuts, just throw them in with the cheese before cooking.

And save butter packets and utensils from the cafeteria.

**Save $20!**
**Simply clip this coupon and give it to your date.**

Sorry, not paying for your dinner this time, toots.

And I use my Frisbee as a plate.

# How to
# Build a BBQ Grill
## . . . To Impress Your Hobo Friends

Did you know that hundreds of people die each year because they are unable or too lazy to clean off their BBQ grills? Well, not really, but this grim outcome might become a horrible reality if more Americans like you don't chip in and build your own grills.

I worked at Sears for a summer, and I told most customers, "Look, old man, you should really build your own grill/riding lawnmower/gift wrap." Needless to say, if these customers had taken my advice, we would have less hunger in America, and a whole bunch less people in the complaint line at Sears.

Before you lose the last of your precious stamina, make yourself a grilling machine. It's great for all of those hardcore football parties you hold on Sundays in your backyard with your favorite stuffed animals...err... friends.

DID YOU KNOW...
The BBQ Grill is the Time-Tested Way to Dispose of Evidence.

Kingsford charcoal begun by using discarded wood chips from Model T Ford plants. That's similar to the innovation you show when hanging out behind a Chinese restaurant, begging for scraps.

If you grill it, it looks nothing like rat.

# Getting Started

**Cost:**
Under $10

**Difficulty:**
The most difficult part will be not burning yourself.

**Time:**
Couple-a-hours

**Stuff You Need:**
- Baking Pan (as deep as you can get)
- Bag of Charcoal
- Roll of Aluminum Foil
- Oven Rack
- 5 Bricks or Cinder Blocks

Making a barbecue grill out of household items will impress anyone you're feeding, even your pets. This is a great one for a day at the beach or park, but not a theme park or kindergarten.

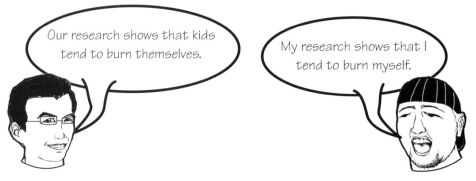

Our research shows that kids tend to burn themselves.

My research shows that I tend to burn myself.

**1** Hopefully you have an oven. Open it up and look inside. There should be a nice rack.

I like nice racks!

**2** Remove the rack. That's the grill.

3

Then you need to create a container for red hot coals. You can use the baking pan, but if you want to be able to use the pan ever again, liberally cover the inside of the pan with foil.

4

Set up your barbecue outside in a safe place, on something nonflammable. The pan is going to get very, very hot, so ideally that means on top of bricks, or cinder blocks.

**5** Next, you'll need to position the grill so it hovers above the coals, for instance by using more bricks stood up horizontally along the edge that stand higher then the top of the pan.

**6** Place the grill on top of the bricks. Make sure that everything is very, very stable.

# 7

Now pour in the coals and start your fire. Once the coals are red hot, place the oven rack grill on top and start cooking. Yeah!

## Beer Can Chicken Recipe
### Ingredients
Whole small chicken (7 lbs.)
Quarter-full beer can.
### Directions:
Remove giblets, pin the wings. Figure out how to fit the chicken in the upright beer, and grill it on medium for about 80 minutes.

# How to Build A Solar Oven
## . . . For the Meat Craving Hippie

Anyone who remembers camping as a kid knows that the worst part is when your Irish coffee gets cold. Scientists have studied this problem for years, and have decisively concluded that it occurs because camping is stupid. We believe camping was invented by cavemen.

The Romans have been using solar ovens for 2,000 years. You know what else the Romans did 2,000 years ago? Massive orgies. The connections are obvious.

My dad once stuck his head in a solar oven.

However, if you're unlucky enough to find yourself camping (probably because you're trying to get laid), you might as well make the most of it. You can do this by making sure your hot shit stays hot, and not full of smoky carcinogens. A solar oven is the way to go - not only does it make hot camping drinks like sake or whatever, but it's nearly impossible to burn food in a solar oven.

FUCK YOU EZ BAKE

# Getting Started

**Cost:**
Under $10

**Difficulty:**
Easier than building a lunar oven

**Time:**
Hopefully you're not trying this in winter

**Stuff You Need:**
- 2 Pizza boxes
- Aluminum foil
- Non-toxic glue
- Saran wrap
- Duct tape
- A Stick
- Something to Cook
- The Sun

**1**

Building a solar oven is simple and rewarding. Start by cutting out a window in the top of one of the pizza boxes. Cut to the very back edge of the box and as close to the edges as possible.

**2**

Next, line the inside of the box with aluminum foil, with the shiny side up to maximize reflection. Glue the foil down, but be sure it's a non-toxic glue.

**3**

Then line the window with Saran wrap, pull it taut and duct tape it down along the edges.

If glue is toxic, why is it so delicious?

**4**

Cut the lid and back off the other pizza box. Line the bottom of that lid with aluminum foil (but not on the extra little back flap) and glue it down.

*A Word to the Wise:*
Don't look directly at the sun. It'll make things more difficult.

## 5

Attach the back flap to the other pizza box with duct tape.

JOKE-A-DAY:
Q: What did the Eskimo say when he went to the sun?
A: The climate here is vastly different than what I am accustomed to!

## 6

Use a stick to prop open the aluminum foil top flap. Adjust the angle to maximize sunlight entering your oven.

Your oven can reach temperatures up to 275 degrees Fahrenheit. That's warm enough to kill germs and to cook up some tasty treats.

If a solar cooker cooks in the forest does anyone give a crap? No. Set up a lounge chair at the beach, or a high-traffic walking area like the mall so chicks will be sure to spot you and ask what the hell you're doing.

The best meals to cook in your solar powered oven include:
* English muffin pizzas
* Hot dogs
* Biscuits
* Snickerdoodle cookies
* Smores.

**Top 5 Other Drunk University Solar Inventions:**
1. Solar powered snow blower
2. Solar powered vampire killer
3. Solar powered bong
4. Solar powered vibrator
5. Solar powered cigarettes

Uh...sorry to be the one to tell you this Mike, but the SOLAR oven won't work inside.

# How to Build
## Ice Shot Glasses
### . . . Melt Away Your Sorrow

Aww crap, it's time to do the dishes. If only there was a way to avoid doing dishes ever again. "Duh, paper plates," you're thinking. You're a quick one! But then you still have to throw out the trash. Not so smart now, are you buckaroo?

Enter: ice. Come on, we both know that nothing is cooler than ice (except maybe smoking cigarettes).

Yeah, solid is definitely my favorite phase of water.

In this episode of "Things Jeremy Does That Are Cooler Than You Do" we will teach you the slickest way to drink shots, ever. Plus, the evidence that you drank all of your roommate's booze will just melt away like an icicle that pierced the heart of a dead man. It's the perfect crime.

# Getting Started

**Cost:**
Under $5

**Difficulty:**
Schmifficulty.

**Time:**
Overnight (so invite a hot friend to help)

**Stuff You Need:**
- Box of 3 ounce Dixie Cups
- Box of 9 ounce Dixie Cups
- Small Tray
- Rubber bands
- Water

$H_2O$, also known as Dihydrogen oxide, was first discovered by Christopher Columbus in 1492 when he drove his car into the ocean blue looking for West Indie Street.

**1** Place as many 9-ounce Dixie cups on the tray as possible. Fill each cup about a quarter inch deep.

Put your tray in the freezer and come back in three or four hours.

**2** When you return, you'll have a bunch of frozen bottoms to your shot glasses. Now place a smaller 3-ounce Dixie cup on top of each frozen bottom. Wrap securely with a rubber band.

**3**

Then fill up in the sides of the 9-ounce Dixie cups with water. See how the 3-ounce Dixie cup interior creates a watery shot glass shape?

Repeat this process for all the Dixie cups and slip the tray back in the freezer.

**4**

Wait three or four hours until the water freezes. Then remove the rubber bands and pour a little warm water into the 3-ounce cups to make removal easy. And if the ice shot glass sticks to the 9-ounce cup, just place it in a cup of warm water a minute to loosen up.

All that is left is a beautiful ice shot glass.

# 6

Now fill up with booze and enjoy!

**Food Network Exclusive Recipe:**
**Apple Shots:**
 **Ingredients**
   **1. Apple**
   **2. Shot**
   **Directions:**
   Cut a 1-inch deep hole into the apple.
   Pour a shot in there; then drink it,
   using the apple as a shot glass.
   Or eat it, freak.

In today's internet-based economy, everything is fast paced. You don't have to wait until you get home to make a phone call, don't have to leave your room to check out the latest movies, and every meal you eat is served through a drive-up window.

With all these new time saving innovations in the world, why are you still imbibing beer with the drinking technology of the middle ages (the mug)? Introducing: our patent-pending Time-Saving Beer Delivery System™, more commonly known as the Beer Bong!

So it's not really patented (shhh!), and yes, the Beer Bong is a classic, but do you know how to build one that will last through your four year college career? No you don't. Not yet, anyway.

But will it last for a six year college career?

Throw away that old, tired oil funnel and retire the pancake batter encrusted, duct-taped contraption you used to think of as a beer bong. We'll teach you how to make an Ol' School Beer Bong, the Defoaming Beer Bong, and a Race Beer Bong.

# Getting Started

**Cost:**
Under $25

**Difficulty:**
Your grandma could pull this off (and drink your pansy-ass under the table)

**Time:**
About an hour

Some people call Beer Bonging "Funneling" but that is just un-original. You're using a freaking funnel for God's sake.

**Stuff You Need:**

Tools:
- Slot Screwdriver
- Razor/Knife/Karate Hand

Materials:
- Funnel
- 4' Tube
- 1 Clamp
- (All of these should be an 1" in diameter or so)

# 1

You are looking for a funnel with a long, straight exit about an inch in diameter. Don't worry if the exit is really long, you can cut it off.

Auto part stores tend to stock these funnels.

**Good! Exit is long and straight.**

**Bad! Exit is short and sloped. Your tube will fall off.**

Long and straight, good? Short and sloped, bad? Where have I heard that before?

Home improvement stores carry all types of tubing. If you're like Jeremy, you'll be fascinated by all the fancy-pants types of tubing but STAY FOCUSED ON THE BEER DRINKING AHEAD!

Buy the tubing that fits tightest on the end of the funnel. When in doubt, buy the narrower tubing with the tighter fit.

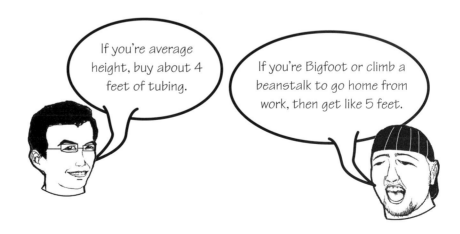

This part is easy. Get a STAINLESS STEEL HOSE CLAMP that matches the size tubing you bought (which matches the size of the funnel opening you bought, which matches your fat mouth, etc).

Don't forget to wash the funnel when you get it home.  And if the exit is longer than 3 inches, cut off the excess with a razor. Ask your lady friends, size does matter.

*Here's a picture of a clamp Dirty Mike drew.*
*You should probably just ask someone at the store.*

## Assembling Your Nuclear Submarine...err...Beer Bong

Ram the vinyl tubing as far up over the funnel opening as it will go.

If the tube is too tight to fit on the funnel opening, boil some water and dip the end of the vinyl tubing in.

Or get a brain transplant and reread the last page...I mean...the hot water will make the tubing very soft and pliable.

Kind of like a fat chick makes my tubing.

**3** Fasten the hose clamp in the middle of the tube stretched over the funnel exit. Tighten the clamp, but lightly.

And of course, check to see if you can pull the tube off of the funnel ...if you can, it's a bad thing.

Wait a second...how come BEER wasn't in the materials?

That's your basic beer bong.
Now we're going to show you how to trick it out.

# How to Build a Beer Bong: With a Valve

The last thing you want to do is walk around with your beer bong like an awkward chump looking for someone to hold it for you.

If you add a valve at the end, looking like an awkward chump will now all rely on your own personal talents.

**\*NEW\* Stuff you Need:**
- Your Ol' School Beer Bong from the last section
- 2 More Clamps
- 1 PVC Threaded Ball Valve
- 2 PVC Threaded Close Nipples

And 1 PVC Threaded Vagina!

At the hardware store, find a 1" diameter nipple that will fit snugly inside your Beer Bong tube.
Grab 2 of these.

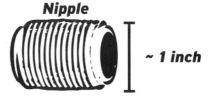

**Nipple**

~ 1 inch

You'll need two more clamps, like the one used in the Ol' School Beer Bong.

Find a threaded PVC ball valve, the same size as your nipples (err...the ones you just bought). Go through the whole box at the hardware store and find the one that's easiest to turn. Or buy them all and decide at home. I don't give a fuck.

DIRTY'S LAW: Beer Bong + Valve = Less Spillage

...about these nipples....
Yes Mike, a small section of pipe is called a nipple.
This one chick I know had nipples the diameter of a pancake.
Excuse me sir, can you tell me where to find the NIPPLES?
If beer came out of my ex-girlfriend's nipples. we'd still be together.
No, we wouldn't.
TOO...MANY... NIPPLE...JOKES!
boom

## ASSEMBLY
## *(Twisting the nipples and all that good stuff)*

**1** Screw the nipples into the valve tightly.

**2** Cut off a 4 inch section of the tube.

**3** Slide the other hose clamp onto the tube.

Use the water trick, if necessary, to make connections.

**4** Slip the end of the tube *not* attached to the funnel, over the nipple.

Hey, it worked on the Iraqis.

**5** Slide clamp over, and make it snug.

**6** Slip a small section of the tubing over the other side of valve.

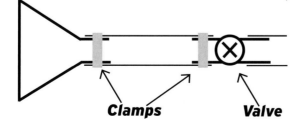

**Clamps**          **Valve**

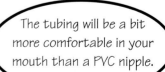

The tubing will be a bit more comfortable in your mouth than a PVC nipple.

# How to Build a Beer Bong: With a Valve & Defoaming System

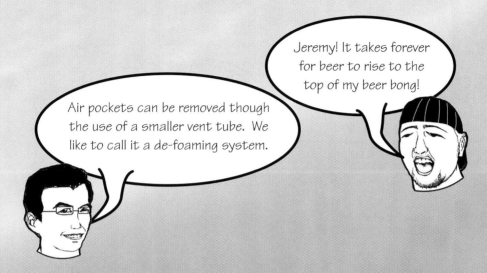

Jeremy! It takes forever for beer to rise to the top of my beer bong!

Air pockets can be removed though the use of a smaller vent tube. We like to call it a de-foaming system.

**\*NEW\* Stuff you Need:**
- Your Beer Bong with Valve from the last section
- Reducing Tee
- Drill + Bit
- Small tubing (1/8" or 1/4")
- Plumbing to attach tube to reducing tee

The plumbing varies by hardware store and depends on the reducing tee you use (so ask).

**1** Insert your reducing tee between the valve and the tubing.

**2** Drill a hole in the funnel.

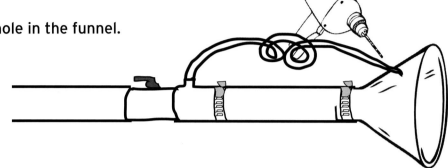

**3** Glue the tube into the funnel.

> I don't think I'm legally allowed to drill anything after "the incident."

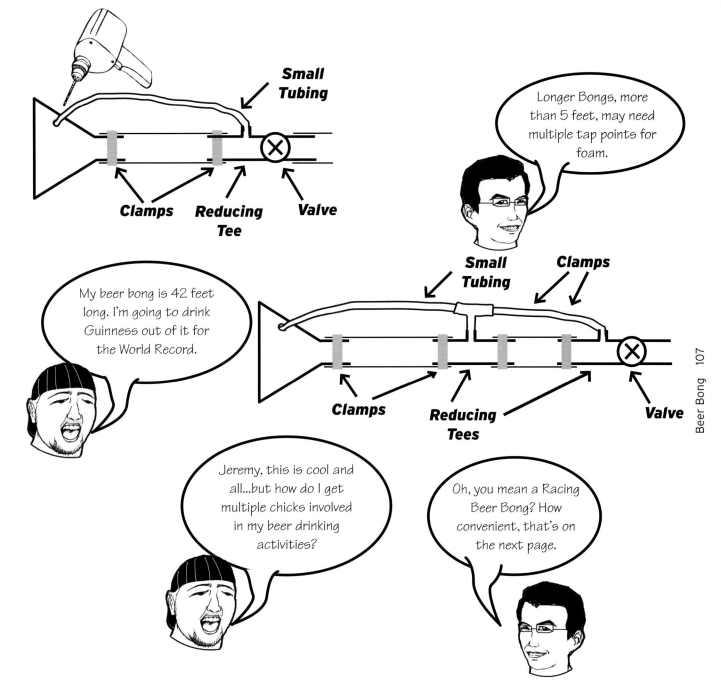

# How to Build a Racing Beer Bong

Drinking in college has gone from the spectators to the athletes. But an athlete is only as good as his equipment.

Multiple person funnel systems vary from the simple double beer bong to a free-standing multiple-person racing machine. Let's begin by learning how to build a two-person racing beer bong.

Note: Read the directions for the Ol' School Beer Bong section before starting this one. That chapter is more detailed because we're not going to print the same info twice.

---

**Stuff You Need:**
- Funnel
- 2 pieces of 4' Tube
- PVC Tee
- 2 90 degree elbows
- 9 Short PVC nipples
- 2 Valves (optional)
- 6  Clamps
  (All should be about 1" in diameter, or fit on that diameter)

---

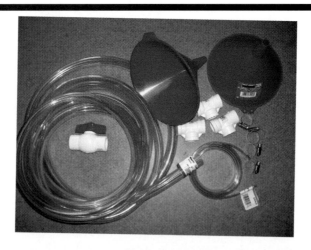

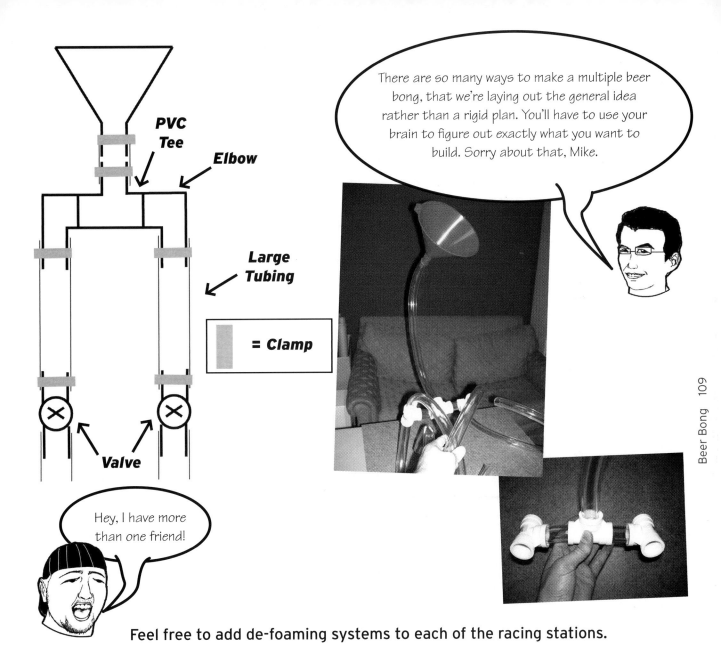

**PVC Tee**

**Elbow**

**Large Tubing**

▮ **= Clamp**

**Valve**

There are so many ways to make a multiple beer bong, that we're laying out the general idea rather than a rigid plan. You'll have to use your brain to figure out exactly what you want to build. Sorry about that, Mike.

Hey, I have more than one friend!

Feel free to add de-foaming systems to each of the racing stations.

It's pointless to add beer past the top of the tubes, as that is "shared" beer and will not count toward the actual race.

## Maintenance:

Wash your damn beer bong.

Rinse after using, and clean monthly with a light bleach solution. Difficult valves can be lubed with Vaseline. Take apart the valve section, and apply Vaseline to the ball of the valve by hand.

Buy extra parts. We know you still won't be as diligent about cleaning as OCD Jeremy, but at least you'll know how to build a new Beer Bong when the old one gets disgusting.

## *Multistory, Tall, and Powered (Compressed Air) Beer Bongs:*

# FOR SAFETY'S SAKE, WE DO NOT RECOMMEND ANY OF THESE TYPES OF BEER BONGS.

Very long beer bongs suction cupped to the windows of a house, hung off of a balcony, a staircase, etc. are dangerous.

BE CAREFUL, as pressure increases by 1 PSI for every 2.3 feet of vertical.

Very tall bongs or bongs powered by compressed air can cause barotrauma of the lungs. It only takes a few PSI.

# How to Build

# An Ice Luge
## ...For the Drunken Eskimo in Everyone

## or . . .How to Make a Bobsled Track for Really Tiny People

The earth is warming and chunks of Iceland are falling into the ocean. So do what Al Gore would do... make an ice luge!

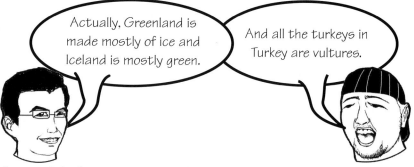

Actually, Greenland is made mostly of ice and Iceland is mostly green.

And all the turkeys in Turkey are vultures.

That's right; there are benefits to global warming. Besides affordable polar bear skin rugs, a giant chunk of ice will transform your drab party into an intense competition where girls will get on their knees and open their mouths . . . for booze, you sick pervs.

Chicks dig artists, right? What better way to impress the ladies than to tell them that you're a sculptor and that ice is your medium? Then you'll have some validity when you ask them to pose for you later that night.

Al Gore's daughters are waaaay hot!

And next time you get invited to a wedding, tell them you'll take care of the ice sculpture center piece. How cool would that be to drink shots off the tail of an ice swan?

# Getting Started

**Cost:**
Around $75 bucks

**Difficulty:**
You just need to be able to spell GED

**Time:**
About two hours

**Stuff You Need:**
- 4ft x 2ft x 2ft Block of Ice
- Friend with a Pick-up Truck
- Butter Knife
- Open Flame
- 2 Towels
- Baking Pan
- Brick
- Strong Table

If you live in an igloo do not use your walls in this project, as it may cause a structural malfunction.

Although the most difficult aspect of this project may seem to be finding a local place where you can buy a giant block of ice, ice is a big business in every city across the nation. Super markets, convenience stores and gas stations all have bags of ice available no matter where you live.

The companies which supply that ice also service bars and restaurants, and they usually have a local ice-making facility that can supply large blocks.

To find that ice maker, go online and type in "ice" and the name of your city, or open the Yellow Pages and look under "Ice." (Hint: However, if you still use the Yellow Pages, you're too old to make an ice luge.)

Okay, start making some calls. If the first ice-maker you call doesn't sell blocks of ice retail then ask them for someone who does. Once you locate a seller, the smallest block they'll probably sell will be a four foot by two foot by two foot block of ice. That's both huge, and heavy. Find a buddy with a pick up truck and lug that glacier home.

If you are hungry on the way back, go through a drive thru...

...stopping at Chuck E. Cheese was a mistake.

Some things to keep in mind:

Ice Melts.
So...

- Buy this party supply last. Ideally, no more than an hour or two before the party begins.
- Do not set up the ice luge in your house.
- Do not set up the ice luge over dirt. It will turn into mud wrestling (See page 190.)
- Set up the ice luge outside on a patio. A children's wading pool can be used as a tub to catch the run off.

**1** Before you carve your ice luge, place towels down on a table, and be careful not to break the block when you lift it up there.

**2** Wrap the brick in a towel and slide it under one end of the ice block, so it has a nice downward slope. The edge of the ice block is touching the table should be resting on a towel. You don't want it to sliding anywhere...and by anywhere I mean off the table.

Next, place the baking pan under the edge of the ice block touching the table to help contain the runoff and melting.

Now here's the fun part: carving the track for the booze to slide down.

You have some options:

- Race track.
  Side by side, straight indentions.
  I recommend this option. Nothing gets a
  party rocking more than some lively competition.

- Winding single track.
  Jamaican Bobsled style. Although this is more fun to
  make, it only allows one drinker at a time.

## *How to carve the indentations into your ice:*

**1**

The simplest way is to heat a butter knife over an open flame. Get it red hot and then gently melt away a path in the ice. You can also use the tip of a heated clothes iron.

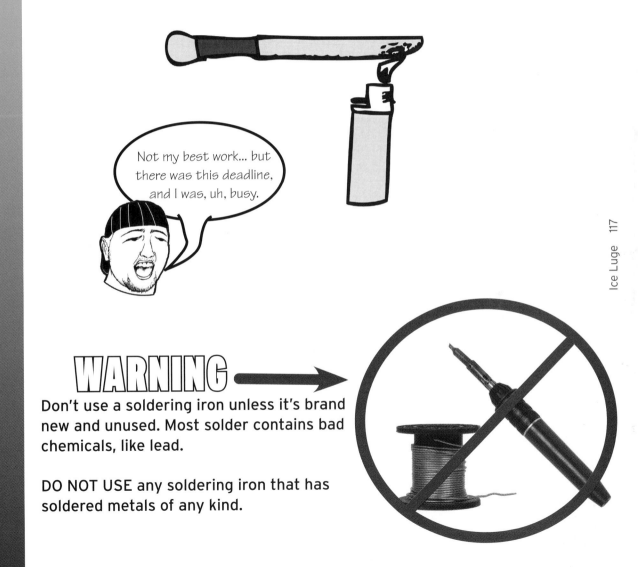

*Not my best work... but there was this deadline, and I was, uh, busy.*

**WARNING**

Don't use a soldering iron unless it's brand new and unused. Most solder contains bad chemicals, like lead.

DO NOT USE any soldering iron that has soldered metals of any kind.

Once a knife or iron has melted a shallow path for the track(s), warm water poured down the track will deepen the chasm.

Your ice luge is ready to party!

This is way better than a Snoopy Sno-Cone Machine!

**ALSO**

Double Block Eight Foot Long Luge: If you want a really huge ice luge, start with two blocks of ice. Push them together and pour a little warm water between them. They will fuse into a MEGA ice luge, like the Mighty Morphin Power Rangers did back when they were still cool.

**History Comes Alive**
The ice luge was first invented in 970 B.C. when teams of Eskimos raced to slurp up spilled Jagermeister.

### *Great Moments in Sports History*

February 11, 1980. After coming in last in the 1980 Olympics, the Botswana luge team sets another record by pouring and pounding ten barrels of whiskey down the icy track.

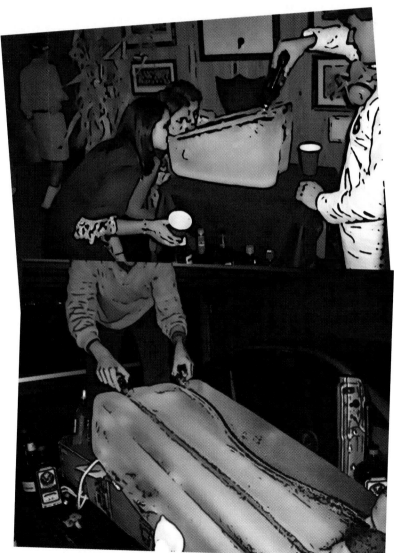

# How to Build
# A Drink Dispensing Jacket
## ...Because You're Too Proud to Spend $5 on Beer

It's game day and after you have already invested $200 on tickets (not counting the ones from that scalper), $10 on one of those giant foam fingers, and $40 on hot dogs, so who wants to pay $5 for a beer?

With the Drink Dispensing Jacket you can guzzle all the booze you can smuggle in, and no one will be the wiser (until you pass out in the second quarter). But be careful, because sneaking in your own alcohol can get you thrown out faster than a bad pick up line on Friday night.

The best part of this project, is that you can fill the jacket with whatever beverage you like. Fill it with apple juice to teach your kids how to stick it to the man at an early age. It doesn't have to be beer or wine, but us health nuts know that more and more studies show that wine has a lot of medical benefits - and after four pounds of ballpark nachos you're going to need all the help you can get.

So grab your rattiest jacket and let's get crackin'.

I have been kicked out of lots of games and I didn't even have the Booze Jacket!

# Getting Started

**Cost:**
Around $30

This will work out to about 35 cents per glass of wine. Makes you want to start buying the stuff regularly, doesn't it?

**Difficulty:**
About as difficult as cutting up a jacket and putting a pouch in it can be

**Time:**
About two hours

**Stuff You Need:**
- Box of Wine (or 1 liter Platypus, or other plastic camel pack)
- Boxcutter
- Old Jacket
- Needle and Thread
- 18" by 18" piece of cloth
- 3' of .5" rubber tubing
- Preferably to the box of wine, you can buy a Platypus plastic Camel Pack (1 liter)

**SMOKER THE BEAR SAYS**

If you fill the jacket with Bacardi 151, you might want to take it off when you smoke.

You have two options on the pouch to use for your Drink Dispensing Jacket.
(1) The Ghetto Way: Empty Wine Box Pouch
(2) The Classy Way: Plastic Camel Pack (for camping)

I would choose the Ghetto Way, but I bet it's more difficult.

## THE MATERIALS

First, the ghetto way.

Skip to Step 3 if you're smart enough to just spend the $20 and BUY THE CAMEL PACK, already.

Warning!!! This project is SO much easier if you just buy a Camel Pack. The box of wine option is described here for the guys who want to build everything themselves and make life difficult.

THE GHETTO WAY
Remove the Plastic Wine Bag from the Box

Here's a step even Mike can handle. It's the simplest step in the history of steps. Cut open one side of the box with the box cutter and remove the wine bag.

Be careful not to cut the bag.

*1*

**3** Next, drain the contents of the plastic bag. Squeeze it to make it go faster.

Leave about 1 liter in the bag if you plan on drinking wine at the ball game.

# Sew a Pocket into Your Old Jacket

Making a pocket is easiest if you choose a jacket with an INTERIOR LINING. That way you don't have to sew in any new cloth. You can just cut a square into the back of the jacket and sew around it if necessary.

You'll want to put the pocket as far up on the back of the jacket as possible. See the dotted box below.

Who do you think I am? Martha Stewart?

**2**

Optionally, you can sew in a zipper so you can open and close the pouch.

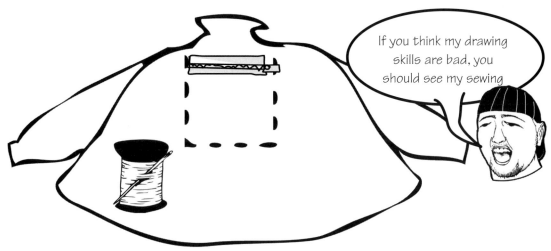

**3**

Within the pocket, sew two pieces of elastic or cloth to hold up the camel pack.

TIP: If you bought the CAMEL PACK (like we told you to) it probably has two little holes you can use to clip up the pack within the jacket.

If you bought the BOX OF WINE, you need to make sure your pocket keeps it in place by sewing it to the right size.

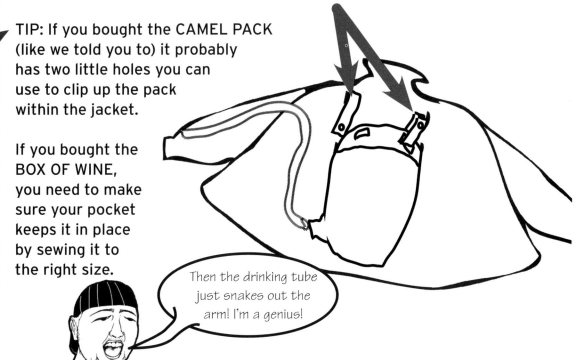

# *Fill that Baby Up!*

Since you don't want to fill your jacket up TOO full, we recommend mixed drinks for maximum punch.

Oh, and if you bought the box of wine you'll need to connect your tubing to the spigot. Make sure it's airtight or it won't work. Good luck.

If you bought the BOX OF WINE...
The box of wine won't come with the convenient little nozzle at your sleeve that is included with the camel pack. After you suck on the wine box tube, you'll need to tie it off with a rubber band on the end, to keep liquid from continuing to flow out.

If you want to drink from your jacket, suck on the tube through your sleeve. To pour a drink, suck on the tube and a natural siphon will be created. As long as you hold the tube below the bag, suction is maintained and the liquid will continue to pour out.

Police Blotter:
9:43 P.M.
Dirty Mike arrested at Costco after pouring 15 bottles of Everclear in his jacket and bloodstream.

# How to Build
## A Beer Shotgunner
### . . . Not for Use on the Road

You're at a party. You bump into some dude on the dance floor and he's like "Watch out, man, before I MAKE you watch out." Are you going to take that?

No, and you don't have to risk a punch in the nose, either. Because you're going to challenge the bully to a drink-off: fastest man to pound a beer wins. Which will be you, because you've attained the superpower of beer shotgunning!

The above scenario is just one of many that can be solved by shotgunning a beer. Such as: your boss wants to fire you for drinking on the job? Challenge him to a drink-off, and collect your raise. A professor accuses you of cheating on an exam? Dispute your grade, challenge him to a drink-off, and whip out your Beer Shotgunner. After you've humiliated him in front of the class, Professor Wuss will be forced to give you an "A."

When you're armed with the Beer Shotgunner a drink-off can solve any number of problems: world peace, anyone?

# Getting Started

**Cost:**
Less than 10 bucks

**Difficulty:**
About a 5 on a scale of 1 to a billion

**Time:**
About 5 minutes

**Stuff You Need:**
- 2" of 1" diameter clear vinyl tubing.
- 10" of 1/8" diameter clear vinyl tubing
- 1/8" drill or small knife

If you've ever tried to chug a full bottle of beer, you know that the beer doesn't move fast, even out of an upside-down bottle. Why? Because air is needed to bubble in to replace the beer flowing out. Breaking this air seal will accelerate beer delivery.

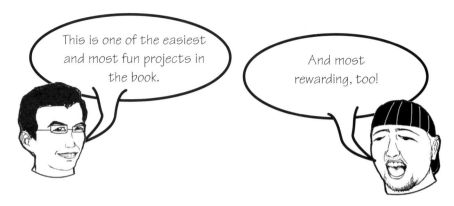

*This is one of the easiest and most fun projects in the book.*

*And most rewarding, too!*

**1** To create your "Bottle Bong" drill or cut a small hole halfway down the larger tube. From the inside of the larger tube, pull about a half-inch of the smaller tubing though this hole.

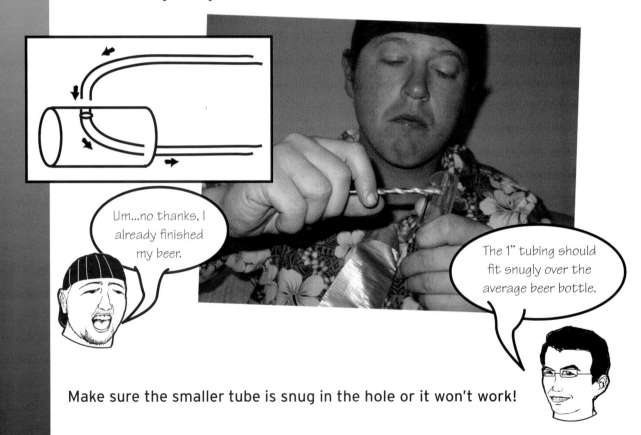

*Um...no thanks, I already finished my beer.*

*The 1" tubing should fit snugly over the average beer bottle.*

Make sure the smaller tube is snug in the hole or it won't work!

**2** Place the small tube inside the bottle.

**3** Slip the large tube over the mouth of the bottle. The small tube should reach most of the way to the bottom of the bottle.

**4** Put your lips over the big tube and pound it!

Spillage Alert: Wear your finest bib the first time you try this.

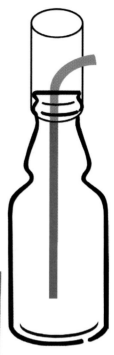

### How it Saves You Time:

Takes 5 minutes to build.

Allows you to pound a full bottle of beer in less than 5 seconds.

This means that if you can normally consume 2 beers in 5 minutes, building this can improve your drinking efficiency by 5,000%!

# The Beer Can Shot-Gunner

### How to Operate Your Can like a Man:

1  Put your mouth over the drinking hole.

2  Opening the tab on the top of the can will break the air seal, and the beer will come gushing out.

**The History of Shotgunning**
This hasn't been tried with soda since 2001 when the extreme beverage, Surge, was taken off the market.

PRODUCT OF U.S.A.

World Famous

12 FL. OZ.

BREWERS GOLD

*Alaskan*

SUN

BEER
LIGHT

Ingredients: water, malt, corn, yeast, hops.

CONTAINS 11% ALCOHOL

SERVE VERY COLD

*Helpful Hints*
Buy a 30-pack and practice at home
before you look like an idiot in public.

You have seen Beer Helmets, but how many Beer Baseball Caps have you seen? A baseball cap that holds beer is much more fashionable...and who needs head protection when you're drinking anyway?

Beer Baseball Caps look so sweet: out of everyone at the party, you'd have the biggest horns. If you were a goat, that's all it would take to get laid. But its horns don't provide the goat with alcoholic nectar, which is why scientists say we're a more evolved species.

This could be you!

It happens all the time, some hot girl wants to make out with you, but you're reluctant to put down your beer. The Beer Baseball Cap solves all that - you can cop a feel and punch out her boyfriend while simultaneously pounding twenty-four ounces of Blatz Ice.

The bigger your hat, the more beer you can pack on it. The Pope could wear a twelve-pack on his hat.

# Getting Started

**Cost:**
$6 (exactly!!!)

**Difficulty:**
Black belt in drinking

**Time:**
About 30 minutes

**Stuff You Need:**
- Baseball Cap
- 2 Gatorade 32 Ounce Containers
- String
- 1/4 Inch Plastic Tubing
- T-connector for Plastic Tubing
- Valve
- Rubber Band

## 1

The plan is pretty simple: attach two Gatorade bottles to your baseball cap, fill them with beer, and run a tube from each bottle into your mouth. Let's get this party started!

The first thing you'll need is a baseball cap.

## 2

All baseball caps have six holes in the cap, you're going to run string through these holes in order to attach the Gatorade bottles, which have two indentations that will help hold the string, one in the middle and one near the bottom.

**3** Cut two pieces of string each about three feet long. Wrap the first piece of string twice around the upper indentation in the bottle, and tie a double knot in the string. Then run the string ends into the cap holes indicated in the photo.

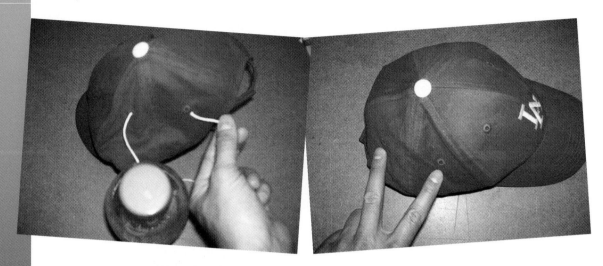

# 4

Tie the string so that the bottle is secured to the hat, and cut off any excess string.

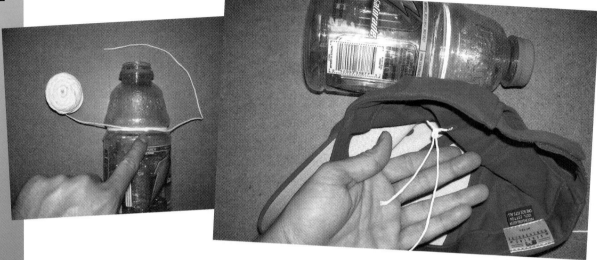

# 5

Wrap the second piece of string twice around the lower indentation in the bottle and tie a double knot.

# 6

Run the ends of the string through the back of the hat, adjust the length of the string, tie a double knot, and cut off any excess string.

**7** Now the bottle should be securely fastened to the baseball cap.
Repeat the process on the other side of the hat with the second bottle.

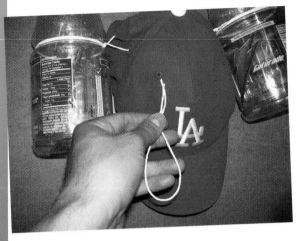

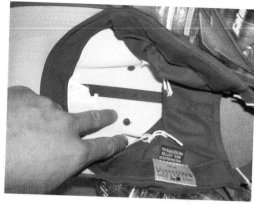

**8** Then, cut two 12 inch pieces of tubing, and drill 1/4 inch holes into the center of the Gatorade tops. Screw the caps back on the bottles, insert a tube into each cap, and connect the tubes with a T-connector.

What sucks about this project, is you'll wish you had Gatorade in the bottles when you wake up with a hangover.

**9** Cut another foot and a half piece of tubing, and attach it to the bottom of T-connector. Add a valve near the bottom of that tube, so you don't waste beer that would otherwise dribble on your shirt.

Never waste beer. That's a sin!

I'm not religious. But yes, it would be a shame to waste good beer.

**10** Next, fasten the drinking tube to your hat. Wrap a rubber band around one of the strings on the underside of the hat, pulling one loop of the rubber band through the other. Then pull the resulting loop though one of the holes at the front of the cap, and string the drinking tube through that rubber band loop.

**11** Nothing left to do, but make a trip to your Keg-o-rator (page 144) and fill 'er up!

# Beer Baseball Cap: For Canned or Bottled Beer

Retrofitting your Beer Baseball Cap for bottled or canned beer is easy. Cut off the top of Gatorade bottles above the middle indentation. Trimmed, the Gatorade bottles are the perfect size to hold a 12-ounce bottle or can of beer.

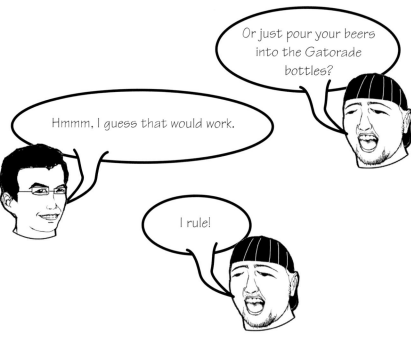

Or just pour your beers into the Gatorade bottles?

Hmmm, I guess that would work.

I rule!

**History comes alive!**
Thomas Edison invented the beer helmet in 1870. He would not make another invention for several decades.

And Moses took a
long glug from his
Beer Baseball Cap.
And the burning bush
spoke unto Moses.
And Moses said,
"Heavy, man!
Leviticus 2:13

Stop being such a baby! You've been childishly squandering your life away, drinking case after case of nasty bottled beer. Real men drink ice-cold draft beer on tap. And don't spend hours going back to the store for more keg ice - that's something little children do.

The Keg-o-rator is the only way to keep a keg cold for a long time. This is especially important if you like breakfast in bed, and what breakfast is complete without a frothing mug of ice-cold keg beer?

With a Keg-o-rator, you'll be able to kick back and relax with cold draft beer on tap at home, while we're hard at work developing a version you'll be able to install in your car.

Here's another plus (or minus, depending on how you look at it): Once you've built a Keg-o-rator, you'll never have a shortage of people at your house drinking your beer.

As soon as I get out of jail, I'm bringing mine to work!

This is the biggest project in the book. It takes more commitment than the average marriage in America these days.

# Getting Started

**Cost:**
$200+

**Difficulty:**
You can't make this.

Don't even try.

But at the very least, you'll learn how to tap a keg properly.

**Time:**
Days. Like 10.

**Stuff You Need:**
• Too much to list. Read on...

In this section, you'll be overwhelmed with more than everything you could ever want to know about kegs. Good luck.

# Beer Delivery Systems

## Taps, Jockey Boxes and Keg-o-rators:

What's the key thing to having a good party? Beer and lots of it.
What other intoxicating liquid can you afford in 15.5 Gallon containers?

General Beer Keg Knowledge:

Full Keg = 15.5 Gallons = 1/2 Barrel
Pony Keg = 7.75 Gallons = 1/4 Barrel
SCUBA Keg = 5 Gallons

KEGS

*7.75 Gallon*
*Pony Keg*

*5 Gallon Cornelius*
*Kegs*

*5 Gallon*
*Keg*

*15.5 Gallon*
*Full Keg*

The tap is an all-in one device. It usually has a hand pump and a tube with a faucet on the end.

The coupler is the device that connects to the keg. A lever controls the center probe, which is pushed down to tap the keg. The lever will lock in down position. Pull on the lever to unlock and untap.

A few couplers are tapped by turning the top 1/4 turn clockwise. The top will lower when turned.

**Coupler types.**
If you have the same taste in beer as Dirty Mike (cheap, common) you probably won't have to worry about an unusual coupler. Although different regions may use different couplers, most American beer kegs use a Sandkey. European beers require a different coupler. Be sure to ask your keg distributor which you'll need when ordering weird or fancy beer.

Where the beer comes out of the faucet, holmes. On the left is what you'll need to build a Keg-o-rator. On the right, a hand-held keg faucet.

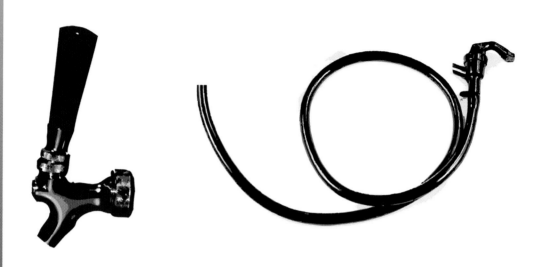

The shank is what the faucet is attached to, which will pass through the wall of whatever the faucet is mounted on. Shanks come in different lengths and inner diameters (bore size), with a nut for the other side to hold them in place.  A beer coupler is attached to supply the beer, and needs to be sized for the thickness of the wall. A 1/2 inch or so of extra shank is necessary to make the beer connection, so don't get a shank that barely makes it though a wall.

A faucet wrench is a special tool for spinning the round coupler that attaches the faucet to the shank. Couplers can usually be turned by hand, but if they get stuck, a faucet wrench will come in handy, and they're cheap enough to buy for that insurance.

A cylinder or tank is a high-pressure container that holds $CO_2$ and other gasses which help push the beer out and keep it carbonated. Connectors vary depending on gas.

### What size $CO_2$ cylinder should I buy?

$CO_2$ Cylinders are measured by how many pounds of $CO_2$ they hold. Steel cylinders are cheaper, but heavier than an aluminum cylinder. For Keg-o-rators, larger is better. Figure 2 to 3 full kegs can be pumped for each pound of $CO_2$ so that means you want as large a cylinder as possible if it will be mostly stationary.

Two gasses are used: Pure $CO_2$ for 95% of all beers. A Nitrogen/$CO_2$ mix is used for some stout beers (like Guinness). This is because beers like Guinness have smaller bubbles and crap. Just trust me.

Anything with a creamy head is a nitrogen-conditioned beer, and will require a special faucet, and a special cylinder is also recommended to ensure the proper mix of the gasses.

You can buy cylinders and tanks at a welding gas supply store, listed under Welding and Industrial Gas Supply in your local Yellow Pages. Some stores may allow you to rent the cylinders for a few dollars a month.

The $CO_2$ regulator converts the high pressure gas in a cylinder to a usable pressure for pumping beer.  It usually has an adjustment screw and two pressure gauges, the lower pressure gauge indicates the output (beer) pressure.  The higher pressure indicates how much pressure is in the tank. One or both of these gauges might be missing on cheaper regulators.

Basically, the larger gauge tells you when you are running out of $CO_2$ and the lower gauge allows you to adjust how much pressure the beer is getting to manage the foam output. As the beer gets lower in the keg, you might have to up the pressure a bit since the beer has to be pumped uphill more to get out to your cup.

CONNECTOR

The beer connector, aka, beer nut Used to connect beer lines to shanks, couplers, etc.  Consists of four major parts:  an insert with a hose barb (host connector part), a nut, a washer, and a clamp which allow for easy disconnection for cleaning, moving or whatever.  They're cheap, and can be bought at any good beer store, or on the internet. Make sure to get the correct size insert/hose barb for your beer tube, and bore size of the shank. Common sizes are 3/16" and 1/4".

Don't stress if the high pressure gauge doesn't change much.  Due to the vapor pressure of the $CO_2$, the pressure will be constant until the tank is pretty much empty.  If your high pressure gauge starts to drop, you need to fill your tank.

### How many gauges do you need?

1:  One gauge will typically tell you the keg pressure, but not the $CO_2$ tank pressure

2:  Two gauges will make you omniscient:  The higher pressure gauge tells the tank pressure, and the lower pressure gauge reads how much pressure is in the keg of beer.

The beer line is the tube that the beer flows through from the keg. Typical sizes are 1/4" or 3/8" inch (inside diameter) tubing. Usually just vinyl tube, but you can get special tube that ensures that your beer taste won't be affected in route to the tap.

The air line is the tube that holds the gas for pressurizing the beer. Typically 5/16" (inside diameter) vinyl tubing, although this size may not be stocked by many hardware stores. You may be able to substitute the more readily available 1/4" tubing, by softening up the end for connection with the hot water, as discussed in the Beer Bong section.

### What should my keg pressure be?

Pressure depends on the length of beer delivery tube, and the height of the exit relative to the beer level in the keg. The easiest way to adjust beer pressure is to set the regulator to 0 psi (Off). Vent all pressure in the keg by holding the pressure relief valve open on the coupler until all air is expelled. While pouring beer, slowly turn up the $CO_2$ regulator until the beer flows nicely, without excess foam.

# Tapping a keg with a pump tap.

**Materials:**
- A hand-pumped keg tap. Rent it where you got the keg, genius.

| Common Causes of Foam | Solutions |
|---|---|
| Dropping or jarring the keg | Get stronger friends |
| Warm beer, not cold enough. (42 degrees is optimum) | More ice |
| Not opening the valve all the way when getting a beer | Laugh at your friends when they pour beer incorrectly |
| Dirty beer system | Take apart and rinse your shit. |
| Too much pressure. Properly pumped/pressurized keg should pour a 10 oz beer in about 4 seconds. | Tell the dude pumping to chill. If you have a $CO_2$ system, turn down the regulator. If pressure is really high, use the relief valve on the keg coupler to let out pressure. |
| Kink in beer delivery tube | Duh. Remove the kink. |
| Ugly chicks at your party | Shut up and keep drinking the foamy beer |

**1**

Pick up the keg early, set it up in the optimal party position and get ice on it a few hours before the party. Try not to drop the keg; which will cause the beer to be foamy for days.

(Note: a full keg weighs about 160 pounds.)

Wait to tap it. I know it's hard to wait for your brew, but tapping the keg when it's either warm, or just been dropped, will produce flat beer.

**2**

Before you tap the keg, make sure the coupler is in the untapped position (handle and center part up). Align the notches in the coupler, and gently place the coupler into the keg and give it a quarter turn until it locks in place. Lower the lever until it locks in, too, and keg is tapped.

**3**

Check beer flow. If no beer flows, pump a few times. When the keg is first tapped, pump sparingly. As the beer level drops, more pumping will be necessary.

If some meathead has already pumped it to the point where the o-ring is jammed, you may have to take apart the pump assembly.

Bronco pumps come apart easily by inserting a coin in the rim and twisting it. Other pumps have a collar on the top that need to be unscrewed. Reseat the o-ring (it fits nicely in the channel). If it's really fucked, the o-ring will be too large for the channel, and it will take some care to get it into place.

**TIP**

***Becoming the hero at your local keg party***
Cheap pump taps aren't reliable, and the pump tends to leak and stick. If this gets to the point where the pump is inoperable, you can be a hero if you find some cooking oil, and pour a bit of oil into the pump. This will lubricate the o-ring inside, and the pump will work again.

## CO2 Party Tap

> **Materials:**
> - A keg, dumbass
> - $CO_2$ Cylinder
> - Fiber washer
> - $CO_2$ Regulator
> - Air Line
> - Handheld faucet
> - 2 hose clamps (same size are the air line tubing)
> - 1 hose clamps (same size as the beer line tubing)

Screw the $CO_2$ regulator onto the $CO_2$ cylinder.  Make sure to include the fiber washer between the two (get it at the same place you filled your $CO_2$ tank).

Connect and clamp (both sides) the $CO_2$ line between the regulator and the keg coupler.

Connect the beer line between coupler and handheld faucet. System should look like this (except to scale...since it will be in real life):

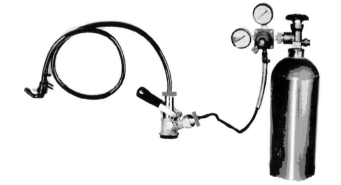

Turn $CO_2$ pressure on, connect keg coupler, engage tapping lever, and drink some beer.

Note:  If you're lazy, you can buy these systems as kits at most beer supply houses, although some kits will include the $CO_2$ tank, and some won't.  (And if you mail-order a $CO_2$ tank, it will be shipped empty.

# *Jockey Box*

Stacking bags of ice around a keg will only keep the beer cold enough not to go bad. If you don't want to settle for anything less than ice-cold beer, get a Jockey box.

A jockey box is basically a cooler with a coil of metal tube inside, and a beer faucet on the side. When the cooler is full of ice, as the beer flows through the tubes, will be chilled from the cool keg, to ice cold.

A jockey box can be purchased assembled for around $200. You could make one yourself, but it will be a royal pain-in-the-ass. However, you might want to assemble your own jockey box, if you find a good deal on a cold plate or a stainless steel coil - but avoid copper coils, they make the beer taste funny.

Putting together a jockey box is very similar to the keg-o-rator construction described later in this chapter. You'll also need a metal ferrule and a rubber grommet to connect the coil to the beer fittings. In the case of a cold plate box, special cold-plate fittings are available. Try to avoid soda fittings, and buy hose barb fittings. Beer tubing can be slid over hose barbs and clamped.

There are several variations on these cold boxes. Some can supply multiple kegs simultaneously, some will have a cold plate inside, instead of a coil of tube. Cold plate boxes are cheaper than coil boxes, but they don't work quite as well, but that's not an issue if the keg is kept slightly colder. Also, the stainless steel cooling coils in boxes can vary in length from a basic 50 foot model to over 100 feet of coil. A 120 foot coil costs almost $200, so figure out if you really want this level of cooling before plunking down two C Notes.

The longer the coil, the more cooling the beer goes through. But beer doesn't get any colder than the ice, so unless the kegs are really warm, long tubes can be overkill. However, if beer is being poured constantly, more cooling will be necessary than if only one beer an hour is being poured.

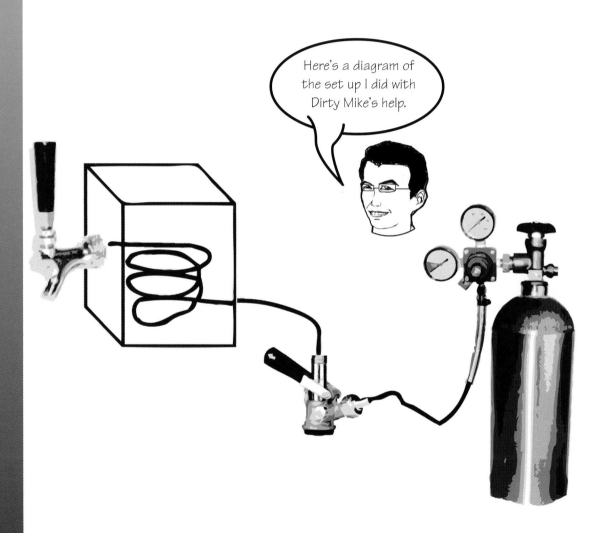

Here's a diagram of the set up I did with Dirty Mike's help.

A pre-assembled jockey box can be substituted for the handheld faucet in the Level 2 system. As shown above, replace the handheld faucet with a standard beer connector tube to the jockey box. Use rubber washers at both ends, and fill the cooler with ice, of course.

Important! Clamp the beer line both at the coupler, and at the entrance to the jockey box. The pressure necessary to push beer though the 50' to 100' of tubing in the jockey box will be much higher than in the previous setup. Expect pressure of up to 35 psi. That much pressure will blow the beer lines off of the connectors if clamps aren't used.

 Jockey boxes are a short-term beer solution for a couple days of partying. At the high pressure necessary to push beer though the tubes, the beer will slowly become over-carbonated.

### Ice management

It's an age-old question: when the ice in the cooler starts to melt, should you drain off the excess water? But in a coil box, the coil is a large vertical appliance, and the water actually will help the cooling process. In a coil box, excess water need only be drained off when adding ice.

On the other hand, a cold plate is a smallish metal pad on the bottom of a cooler. When the ice melts, the water will cause the ice to float away from the cold plate. So, in the case of a cold plate jockey box, leave the ice drain valve open all of the time. This will allow the ice to press down on the cold plate, keeping it cold.

# The Kegorator

Tired of cans piling up? Want fresh beer, anytime?  Tired of unfinished kegs spoiling? A keg-o-rator is the ultimate beer-dispensing system.

---

**But if you'd rather assemble your own Keg-o-rator:**

**Detailed Materials List:**
- $CO_2$ tank
- $CO_2$ regulator w/ shut-off valve and hose barb.
- Air line
- Clamps for air line
- Keg coupler
  (normally comes with $CO_2$ connector but not beer connector)
- Shank
  (sized for beer tube size)
- Beer jumper line
  (Beer line with connectors on both sides.
  It's easier to buy these preassembled.)
- Faucet
- Faucet handle
- Refrigerator

**Tools Necessary:**
- Drill
- 1" Hole saw for beer shank.
- 9/16" Drill for airline (check your tubing outside diameter)

**1**

The first step in assembling your own keg-o-rator is to find a suitable refrigerator. If you buy a used refrigerator from the classified ads, bring along an empty keg, remove the refrigerator shelves and test to see if that model will hold a keg.

Note: Some kegs (such as those for Coors beer) have a bulge in the center, which can cause width clearance problems in refrigerators.

Also, eyeball the fridge for vertical clearance: you'll need head room for the tubes coming off the top of the keg (probably about 6").

**2**

The interior of most consumer kitchen refrigerators get narrower at the bottom, to make room for the compressor motor in the back.
A keg won't fit on the bottom of a consumer refrigerator, because of the little shelf formed by the compressor the door won't be able to close. You'll need to build another shelf that will allow the keg to sit on top of the compressor area.

This will raise the keg but can possibly cause head room problems with the, coupler and beer lines attached to the top of the keg. Allow for at least 5 inches between the top of the keg and the roof of the refrigerator, and another inch for the shelf you'll be building. If the refrigerator you've got doesn't have that 6 inches of clearance, you can buy special "low-profile" keg couplers, but it's still a pain in the ass to fit a keg in a small refrigerator.

For the keg shelf, you'll need 3/4" MDF or 1/2" structural plywood, cut to the size inside the fridge. If you have a hot chick buy it for you, she usually can convince the dude at the lumber yard to cut it to size. You will also need to support the shelf at the front, with either two small pieces of 4"x4," or if you aren't into carpentry, a stack of bricks, or a bundle of 2"x"4's can server as a ghetto shelf.

Next, you'll need to buy all the beer fittings and whatnot. It's best to buy it all at once in a kit: different kits are available depending on whether you want the beer faucet mounted through the door, or the side of the fridge. It may be simpler (and cheaper) to use a handheld faucet inside the fridge, but that means the door will have to be opened to dispense beer, which is kinda lame.

You'll also need to find a place to fill the $CO_2$ tank. You can usually get this done at welding supply stores, soda bottlers, or any other industrial gas supply place. Look on the web for a local place.

Also make sure the shank length is the correct length to fit through the refrigerator wall. Kits usually come with an 8" shank, but that can stick so far out inside of the refrigerator that it gets in the way. A 4"-5" shank is usually about the right length.

You'll need to drill two holes in the refrigerator: one for the shank, and one for the $CO_2$ line.

Be sure to unplug the refrigerator before you drill anything!

The $CO_2$ tank can be kept inside of the Keg-o-rator, but an external tank will work better for easy refill. It's usually best to drill on the side walls, because there are wires and pipes to be avoided running up the back.

Fridge walls are usually plastic on the inside, metal on the outside, with insulation sandwiched between. This can be tricky to drill so make sure to check for wires and/or pipes after getting through the first layer of drilling. You wouldn't want to accidentally bust any of the internal workings of your fridge.

**6**

I usually drill the $CO_2$ line hole in the side near the back, which is a good place to put the $CO_2$ tank for appearance and accessibility purposes. The hole should enter at about keg height, so the tube doesn't get pinched by the keg. The shank (which connects to the beer faucet) can be inserted either in the door, or the side of the refrigerator. I prefer the side, otherwise the beer line will get pinched in the door when it's opened. All your friends will want to look inside of your Keg-o-rator, so unless you're planning on padlocking the door, it will get opened a lot at parties. Also, stuff can be put in the refrigerator around the keg, and you won't be able to pour beer while the door is open (unless the faucet comes out of the side of course).

Oh, and please unplug your refrigerator when you drill it.

**7**

Lastly, if you use a bucket as a drip tray, it will get moved every time the door is opened. Drunk people will forget to put the bucket back, and beer will drip all over your floor.

### Clean your beer lines

Just as with the Beer Bong, you'll have better tasting beer if the faucet, coupler, shank, and jumper are cleaned after each time after keg is finished. This is especially true if the Keg-o-rator has been turned off for a period of time between kegs. Special beer line cleaner is available, but rinsing everything with hot water works just as well. I'd advise you to take the faucet and coupler apart and wash inside every couple months. (A special faucet brush will cost only a few bucks from the beer supplier.)

Use the hole saw to drill a one inch hole for the shank (in either door or side of refrigerator.) Insert the shank into the hole, and secure it with the supplied nut. Screw on the faucet. Connect your beer jumper line to the coupler and the shank. Pull the $CO_2$ tube through it's hole, and attach it to the coupler with a clamp. You are now ready to put a keg into this bad boy. (But if a refrigerator has been moved, or turned on its side, wait a few hours for the lubricant to settle. Plugging a refrigerator in immediately after handling can cause damage to the motor.)

**WARNING**
If your Keg-o-rater gets hit by lightning, it may come to life as a really drunk robot.

Authors' Note:
Some people write Keg-o-rator, others write Kegerator.

In our original text for this book, we spelled it both ways throughout,
but we are told that it would make this already confusing section more
confusing - and was making our proofreader furious.

# THE WEEKEND
## PARTYING

# How to Build
# A Foam Gun
## . . . Not For Use in Duels

Have you ever wondered how to achieve more female nakedness at your parties? Who hasn't wondered, right? Well, it's real simple: add water. Even better? Add soapy water.

And what do you know, we've designed a gun that will spray foam all over a dance floor, wrestling pit, or your grandma's Thanksgiving dinner.

Remember the good ol' days when you played in the bubble bath with a rubber ducky and didn't have a care in the world?

Unfortunately, those days are over. But with our foam gun you can force others to experience the magic of bubbles. In the process, we guarantee you'll forget all about little Ducky-poo.

Even better than soapy water is all-pervasive foam. No white t-shirt will be left with even a hint of opacity.

# Getting Started

**Cost:**
Around $60

**Difficulty:**
Depends on how easy it is for you to find a leaf blower, cheap

**Time:**
About an hour

**Stuff You Need:**
- 1 Inch Hole Saw Wood/Drill
- Leaf Blower
- Plastic shower puff (That puffy thing chicks use to clean themselves) or raw screen material (from a screen door, or you can buy this crap at a hardware store)
- Several two liter bottles

# 1 Get an old leaf blower...

Choosing a Leaf Blower:
First, buy a used, cordless leaf-blower off Craig's List.

New leaf blowers are like $100 or something.

So buy a used one.

A gas-powered leaf-blower will be way too loud and smelly. A cordless leaf blower is best and safest (since you'll be blowing water out of the thing).

# 2 Create Your Soap-Water Mixture

Ingredients for Your Soap/Water Mix:
Dishwashing soap foams up nice, but can be hard on the eyes.  Baby shampoo is best on eyes and skin, but can foam down fast.

Jeremy recommends 1 CUP of soap for 1 GALLON of water.

Here's something Dirty Mike doesn't know much about: soap and water.

That's more soap than I've used in my entire life.

Dirty Mike can feel like an engineer (and so can you) by experimenting to find the best soap to water ratio, with different soaps.

## 3 *Let the Foaming Begin!*

Drill a 1 inch hole about half-way down the blower nozzle. Then, stuff the end of the blower with either a plastic shower puff or the screen material.

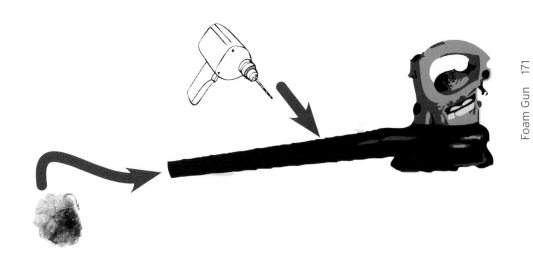

**4**

Fill the 2-liter bottles with the soap/water mixture.

I never knew soap could be so useful!

**5**

Flip the leaf blower up-side down and jam one of the 2 liter bottles filled with soapy water into the hole you drilled.

**6**

Turn on the blower, and turn it right-side up, tipped downward.  Foam will blow out the end.

# CAUTION

Avoid tipping the blower up!
Soapy water is not a good mix with technology and stuff.

**GOOD**

**BAD**

# How to Build
# A Laser Light Show
## . . . Or Blind Several People at Once

You've seen them in movies, on television, and during presentations. That's right, I'm talking about freakin' lasers.

I know what you're thinking. "Lasers used to be cool, back in the '70s when they were in that one movie my parents always talk about." Well, you're wrong. Lasers are making a comeback.

Don't you watch music videos? Lasers will turn a drab party where everyone is sitting around playing Scrabble into a scantily clad, sweaty dance party with a live performance from 50 Cent.

What was that movie called? Star Battles?

And what about movies? No Super Villain these days can get away without at least a world-exploding laser or two.

So run on down to the discount bin at Office Depot, or wherever you typically do your laser shopping, and prepare yourself for the LASER LIGHT SHOW.

# Getting Started

**Cost:**
Around $50 bucks

**Difficulty:**
Some high school required

**Time:**
About two hours

**Stuff You Need:**
- Speaker or Stereo System w/ Uncovered sub-woofer, or an old woofer
- 1-3 Small Mirrors (steal these from your sister)
- 1-5 Laser Pointers
- Superglue / rubber glue
- Tin foil

The more lasers and mirrors the better, but at a certain point you might as well buy a disco ball.
Hint: Just buy a disco ball.

**1**

Glue a chunk of mirror near the cone (center part) of the speaker.

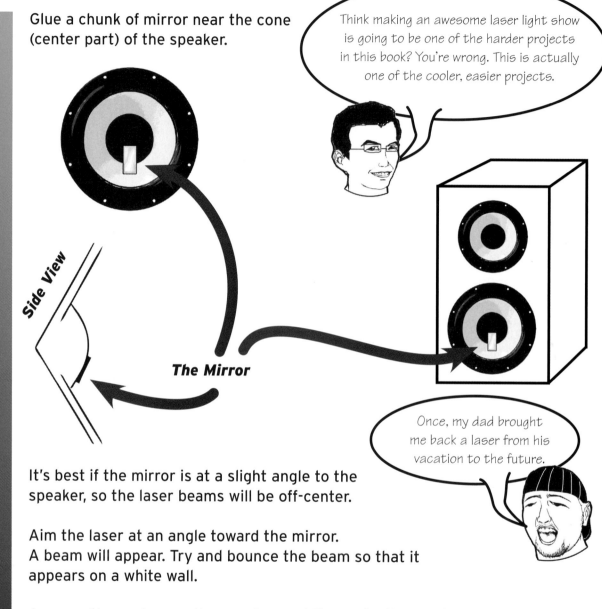

Think making an awesome laser light show is going to be one of the harder projects in this book? You're wrong. This is actually one of the cooler, easier projects.

*Side View*

*The Mirror*

Once, my dad brought me back a laser from his vacation to the future.

**2**

It's best if the mirror is at a slight angle to the speaker, so the laser beams will be off-center.

Aim the laser at an angle toward the mirror.
A beam will appear. Try and bounce the beam so that it appears on a white wall.

Arrange the system so the speaker and the projection surface are as a far apart as possible. The longer the distance between the two, the larger the patterns in the light show will be.

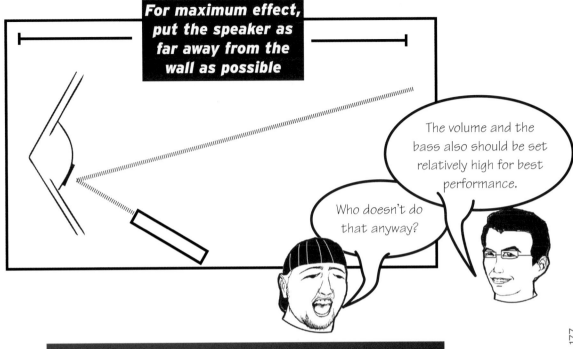

3 Set up the show so the laser beams are well above, or below, eye level (project them onto the ceiling, if possible). Just to be safe, avoid nose level, too. You can lean the speaker against something or adjust the angle of the laser.

**Remember when...**
you watched that video with J-Lo and all the green lasers, but ignored the girls gyrating and thought "Cool! Lasers!" You were 12 years old.

There are four ways to increase the awesomeness of your laser light show:
#1 Add More Lasers
#2 Add Colored Lasers
#3 Add More Mirrors
#4 Add More Speakers

#5 Paint racing stripes on your speaker.

DANCE WITH CONFIDENCE!!!

Lasers...they're not just for ruining other peoples' movie-going experiences anymore!

Yeah, grow up dude.

**TIP**

Green Laser Pointers: If you have the bucks, try to get a green laser pointer. These cost abou* $100, but will increase the range of your show. Think about hitting the sides of warehouses, even clouds, with a high-powered green laser pointer.

But how will this protect my home from terrorists?

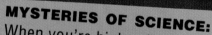

**MYSTERIES OF SCIENCE:**
When you're high... flashing, colored lights are great when they're coming from a laser pointer. Yet, mysteriously, they're not as enjoyable when coming from a cop car.

***The Laser Haiku:***
Laser beam space ship
Zapping all the aliens
Galactic hate crimes

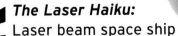

# How to Build
# A Super Slip and Slide
## . . . Not for Children Under 18

Remember Slip 'n' Slides? These things were fun to buy, fun to set up, and completely boring to use. About 15 minutes after this was invented, everyone figured out you could just line up a bunch of wet garbage bags to make a waaaay better and practically free slide. You'd run at top speed, jump, and slide on the gummy plastic until you slid off and your trunks fell off covering your private regions with severe grass burns.

Fun, but not fun enough.

Our "fun experts" demand more: a life-threatening experience, followed immediately by a death-defying act. That's the definition of summer fun.

Our Super Slip 'n' Slide takes you downhill at amazing speeds of up to 10,000 inches per hour! Then, you're launched in the air at a dizzying height of three feet, and plunged into a pool of heated water. Yeah, that's what fun is.

Don't slide head first if you want to keep passing your classes.

# Getting Started

**Cost:**
Like $40 bucks

**Difficulty:**
There are 5 levels. They get cooler, but also exponentially harder.

**Time:**
From 30 minutes to 5 hours.

**Stuff You Need:**
- Plastic sheeting
- Garden hose with running water
- Dish Soap (Optional)
- Sandbags or old carpeting (Optional)

Slip 'n' Slide was first invented by the scientists at Wham-O, who got the idea when they saw a little boy with a dislocated shoulder.

# Simple Slip 'N' Slide

Plastic Sheeting
This can be purchased at most hardware stores in rolls of 10 by 100 feet and is usually located in the paint department by the tarps. One hundred feet is a lot, and can be used for several slides.
The thicker sheeting the better.

Find a grassy hill.

Spread the tarp out the long ways down the hill.

Put the hose with running water at the top.

Slide down.

Flat areas are for pussies.

I like 6 mils (a mil is a thousandth of an inch) but 3 mils will do.

If the water isn't running down the center of the slide, put sandbags or a roll of old carpeting down each side of the slide to contain the water. Tuck the ends of the plastic under the sandbags/carpet. This will help keep the slide in place.

If the slide isn't fast enough for your taste, add a splash of the dish soap: this will speed things up. Still not fast enough for you, zippy? Find an old body board with a smooth bottom. Go down on that bad boy.

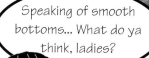

Speaking of smooth bottoms... What do ya think, ladies?

# A Jump

Arrange the jump by placing the sandbags under the sheeting most of the way down the hill. If your slide has running water make sure the jump launch ramp is properly sloped (see diagram below), or water will pool and slow you down.

Ideally, pad the landing with some carpet or foam.

**Additional Materials:**
More sandbags or carpeting
Anything that is soft can be used.

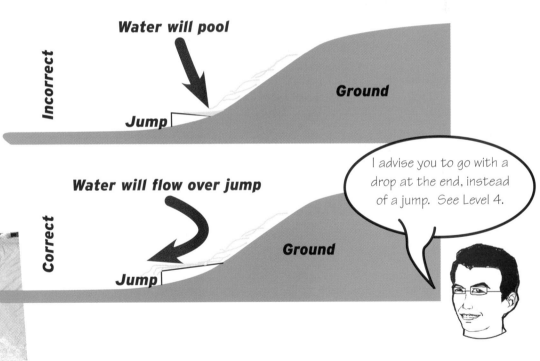

Incorrect

Water will pool

Jump

Ground

Correct

Water will flow over jump

Jump

Ground

I advise you to go with a drop at the end, instead of a jump. See Level 4.

# A Bank

Stack up sandbags to make a banked turn. Remember not to create any areas for water to pool. This means that at every part of the bank, the slide should have a slight downward angle.

**Additional Materials:**
Lots of sandbags

# A ramp with drop into a pool

Unless you can find a hill that empties into a natural depression, having standing water in a pool of some sort at the end of the slide is tricky because water will not climb

over the side of the pool. That, and you'd slide into the side of the baby pool. The solution is to build a ramp. These ramps are similar to skate ramps.

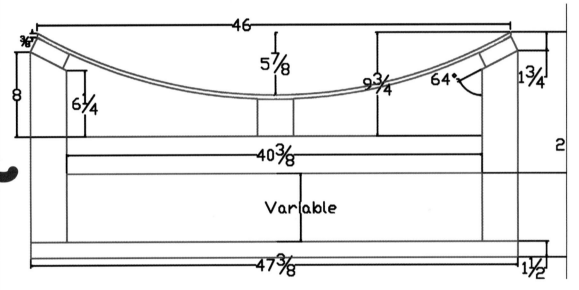

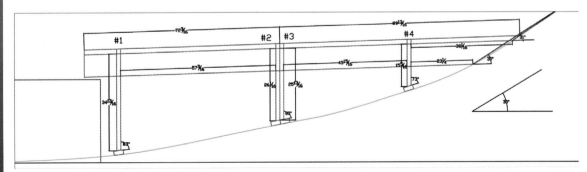

This model is constructed from 2"x4"s and 3/8" plywood (The center board is a 4"x4", a bit of overkill). After the frame is constructed, soak the plywood in water, and set in the sun.

Have several friends stand on the plywood to hold the curve down, and tack it into place.

Staple carpet on the top of the plywood for padding. The plastic sheeting is then laid over the top of the carpet, and stapled around the sides.

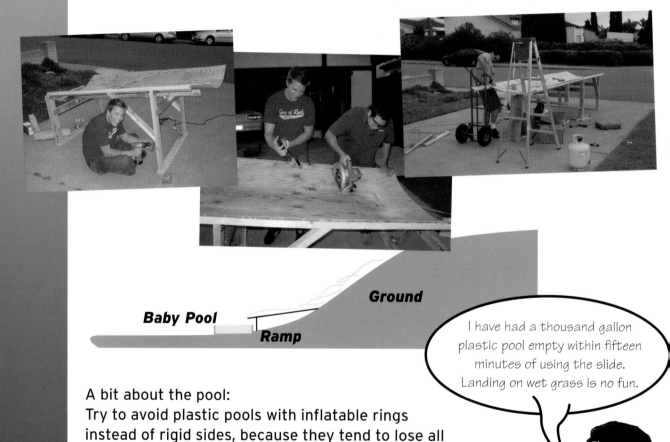

A bit about the pool:
Try to avoid plastic pools with inflatable rings
instead of rigid sides, because they tend to lose all
of their water rapidly when exposed to the level of waves
caused by people falling in off the slide.

I have had a thousand gallon plastic pool empty within fifteen minutes of using the slide. Landing on wet grass is no fun.

# Recirculating Water

If you've gone to the trouble to build a ramp emptying into the pool, the fun can be increased by upping the amount of water cascading down the slide.

**Additional Materials:**
Pool / storm pump
Appropriate hose for the above pump
Strainer for above hose

Locate the pump very near the bottom of the pool. Pumps will always push water better then they suck it.

*Most hoses can't put out that much water, but a pool pump can.*

*Pumps don't make good girlfriends...*

Once you've procured the pump, put the suction end in the pool. The suction end needs to be a few inches underwater at all times. If the suction end nears the air, the pump will suck in air, and stop working.

As people splash down from the slide huge waves will be created in the pool, and if the wave exposes the suction line, even briefly, the pump will suck air.

*Install a strainer on the suction end, especially if using a pool pump. Or the grass tracked into the slide by all of the users will rapidly clog a pump (trust me).*

A strainer isn't as critical with gas-powered storm pumps because they deal with grass and debris much better.

# Heating Water

Most insane waterslides are a very male affair. Using warm water on your slide will increase female participation, a very good thing, especially if said females are wearing white t-shirts?

Get a hold of an old gas Jacuzzi heater setup to burn propane. (All gas appliances have a badge near the gas inlet which should specify what gas the heater is setup to burn and how many for how many BTUs.)

**Additional Materials:**
- Old Jacuzzi Heater (Preferably one setup for propane)
- Propane Tank
- BBQ propane regulator
- Someone who's handy

*Girls like to complain that the water is too cold.*

*Talk to the guy at the pool store before you attempt this. It's way too complicated to describe in detail here, but I'll go over the basics.*

If your Jacuzzi heater is setup to burn natural gas, don't use it unless a gas technician has converted it to propane use by changing the gas nozzles. Natural gas has less than half the energy than propane does per volume, and if a natural gas heater is hooked to a propane tank it will create more than twice the heat than it was designed for and could melt, or cause a major fire.

Next, buy a propane regulator (they can also be found on BBQ's, turkey fryers, and almost anything to which a propane tank is attached.) Hardware stores will also sell replacement regulators to these appliances: you want a regulator rated for the same BTU's as the heater. Attach this to the gas input of the heater.

Hook the heater in the water recirculation loop after the pump. Hook the propane tank up, light the pilot, start the pump, and turn on the heater.

# How to Build
# A Mudwrestling Pit
## . . . Dirty + Water = Sexy?

Many people think female mud-wrestling is a sexist sport. Not true: it combines two of a woman's favorite pastimes: fighting other women and looking sexy.

Like beer goggles, a mud wrestling pit is a great way to make so-so women appear super-attractive. Not only that, but hot women tend to want to fight other hot women, for Highlander-esque reasons. An even better movie analogy is *Field of Dreams*: build a mud-wrestling pit and chicks in bikinis will come to your backyard, as if by magic.

Want to take your party to the next level? Is foam too clean? Try a mud wrestling pit.

Be sure to cover your mud-wrestling pit at night, otherwise you might wake up to an infestation of swimsuit models.

# Getting Started

**Cost:**
Um...are you stealing the sand or buying it?

**Difficulty:**
It's probably too hard a project for you; you don't want to see semi-nude women wrestle, anyway.

**Time:**
An hour

**Stuff You Need:**
- 50-100 Sandbags
- Large Tarp
- Mud

The world's largest mud-wrestling pit is the Florida Everglades.

# *A Simple but effective Mud Pit*

Sandbags are ideal for making a small berm, that won't bruise your semi-nude contestants when they're slammed into the side of the pit.

Arrange the sandbags in a ring, by stacking them in an alternating pattern for strength, at two or three levels height.

Stretch the tarp over the ring of sandbags. Tuck the ends of the tarp under the ring of sandbags. Fill with mud. Have fun.

## *A tad too cold for mud wrestling? Try a heated pit.*

If you have a washtub in your laundry room, a hose can usually be attached to the sink spigot. Run the hot water out a window/door to the pit, and voila, hot mud.

If you don't have a wash tub, you can draw warm water directly from your hot water heater, which has a drain valve at the bottom to which a hose can be attached.

Drain a few gallons out the heater before connecting the hose to your pit. There's usually a certain amount of sludge at the bottom of a hot water heater, because most people don't often drain their heaters.

Mud Wrestling? When we say mud wrestling, we mean you can fill your pit with any messy substance, from mud to Jello. Viable wrestling substances include mud, clay, gelatin, jelly, oil, sex lube, pudding, ramen noodles, soup, corn, and mashed potatoes. We're big fans of pottery clay, which can be watered down to a perfectly soupy mud (with no rocks in it.)

FACT! Mud clears the pores. This is why mud wrestling chicks are so unbelievably HOT!!!

# How to Build
# Party Lights
## ... That Dance to the Music

Unlike you, these lights are always on beat.

Alright, here's the 555-1212:
These Christmas lights will flash in time with your stereo music. Take a minute to clean your brains off the wall, and then read on. There are many great advantages to in-tempo flashing lights, even when you're not totally wasted. For instance, it's a widely known fact that supermodels are hypnotized by shiny, flashing things. You can set up a string of these in your backyard, and trap a dozen supermodels by the end of the evening.

But that's not all! It's a documented phenomenon that dance floor lights, flashing in-tempo, increase booty shaking by 40%. That could mean the difference between a meager little jiggle and full-on trunk poppin'!

This year, I'm going to ask Santa for Christmas lights instead of a girlfriend.

# Getting Started

**Cost:**
Around $10 bucks

**Difficulty:**
Easy-peasey. If you can jump-start your car without seeing angels, you'll do fine.

**Time:**
About an hour

**Stuff You Need:**
- Stereo System
- String of Cheap Xmas Lights (not-LEDs)

These are the second best way to pep up your family Christmas gatherings, next to Ecstasy.

**1** The cheap sets of Xmas lights are wired in a big loop. Cut the plug off the end of lights.

**2** Cut into two sections of 10 lights. If you have a small stereo, reduce this number of lights to 6.

**3** Connect the ends of the loop to the "B" or "remote" speaker outputs of your stereo

**4** Enable the B speakers on your stereo, and play some music.

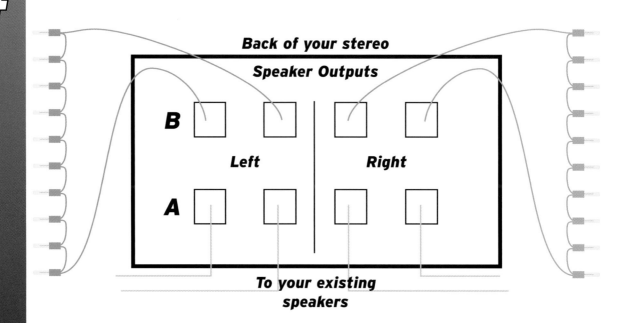

**Back of your stereo**

**Speaker Outputs**

**B**

**Left**        **Right**

**A**

**To your existing speakers**

# Number of lights to use.

**KNOW YOUR PARTY LIGHTS:**
White party lights: Frequently off-beat
Red party lights: Make everyone look like a Dutch window-hooker
Yellow party lights: Make it impossible for chicks to know you have jaundice
Silver party lights: Turn piles of puke into really shiny-looking piles of puke
Black party lights: Are really hard to see

## WARNING!
Party lights may refuse to dance to country music

# Add Xmas Lights to Your Car

Yeah, yeah. Can I take these on the road? I get so bored when I'm driving sober.

A complete set of Xmas lights would run very dim in a car, but if you reduce the number of lights it will work. For a 12V car system, wire 5 bulbs into a cigarette lighter plug, which can be purchased at most auto parts stores.

# How to Build
## A Traveling Stripper Pole
### ...For Anyone Besides Your Mom

Want to keep your stripper pole in the garage until the kids are put to bed? Or take it to your high school reunion and demonstrate your new profession right on the spot?

The Traveling Stripper Pole is actually a codename for Operation: Stripper Pole Not Mounted into the Ceiling. Your mission, if you wish to undertake it, is to get as many sweet, innocent, young ladies as you can to strip for you to songs like the Macarena (*editor: please replace with whatever is "hip" nowadays*).

This thing is easy as hell to build, and considering the thousands of dollars it will save you on trips to the strip club, you can't afford not to make it.

My ceiling already has enough holes in it.

This stripper pole can be easily moved in a friend's truck.

# Getting Started

**Cost:**
About $100

**Difficulty:**
Easier than convincing the girlfriend to let you go to the strip club. But seriously, you need some carpentry skills for this one.

**Time:**
3 hours

**Stuff You Need:**

Tools You Will Need
- Drill, drill Bit (2 inch)
- Skill saw
- Hammer
- Screwdrivers
- Wrench

Parts you'll need:
- 2 Sheets of Plywood (1" thick)
- Steel Pole (threaded)
- Matching Flange
- Twelve Foot Beam (4" x 4")
- 4 Bolts, Washers, & Nuts
- Nails

FACT:
The easiest way to fill your house with strip-teasing women is to advertise as an Aerobics Studio.

**1**

There are two parts to the Portable Stripper Pole: the pole and the part that will keep the pole connected to the ground.

For the pole, you'll need a piece of steel pipe that is threaded on one end. You'll screw the pipe into the flange and bolt the flange down onto a wood base.

**2**

Standard ceilings are eight feet tall, so the pipe you buy should be about seven and a half feet in length.

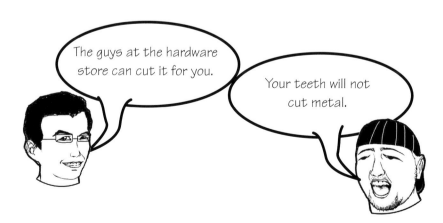

The guys at the hardware store can cut it for you.

Your teeth will not cut metal.

You'll be making a mini stage to house your stripper pole, so you'll need two pieces of plywood -- one for the base and the other for the stage.

Wood can be expensive, but the thicker the better. Half inch thick plywood is too thin; buy plywood at least 3/4 inch thick.

Bolt the flange to the base board. Use washers on the bottom of the base so that the wood won't rip.

Although I would recommend 1 inch thick.

**Nut**

**Flange**

**Plywood**

**Washer**

**Screw**

If you've followed the instructions so far, you should have a piece of plywood with a flange attached and a pole that can be screwed in.

Perfect.

3

**1**

Drill a hole in the piece of plywood that will be acting as your stage, where the stripper pole will pass though.

Make sure that the hole is perfectly lined up with the flange and that the hole isn't too big. We want the pole to barely squeeze through.

**2**

Next you'll need to build the frame of the stage. Depending on your carpentry skills, you can make this as tall and intricate as you desire. But for the quickest and simplest version, cut a 4" by 4", twelve foot beam into twelve, foot long pieces.

**3**

With the pole removed, nail four of those pieces to each corner of the base, four at the center of each edge, and four evenly spaced by the flange.

**4**

Place the stage on top and nail down securely. Insert the pole into the hole. Screw in tightly. And enjoy.

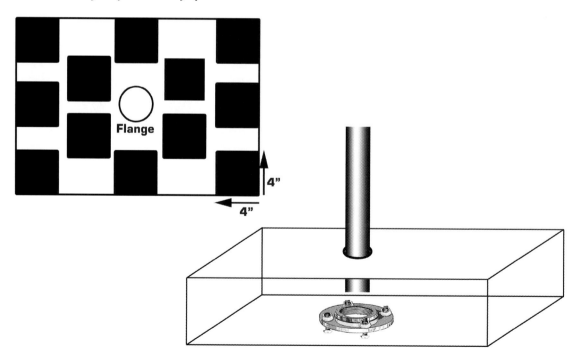

Flange

4"

4"

Set up your stripper pole at someone else's party. When there are 4 or 5 hot babes latched on, have a friend with a crane carry the stripper pole back to your house.

Feeling Generous? Rent or loan your stripper pole to a local charity for an easy fundraiser. And they say you have no morals.

*"I Thought I Told You That We Won't Stop"*

Get kicked out of the strip club again? Start your own strip club in the parking lot!

# TOO MUCH TIME ON YOUR HANDS

## FUN & GAMES

# How to Build
## A Fatty Detector Mat
### . . . So You Don't Have to Hide the Cake

Ever since roaming nomadic tribes of hunter gatherers first met up for festive celebrations, there's always been a question that plagued even the wisest of homo sapiens: how to improve the fatty to hottie ratio?

Any doctor will tell you that the most important part of curing a problem is early detection, and sure they were talking about cancer, but the principal still applies. We introduce to you to: the Fatty Detector Mat!

You won't have to hide the chips, or tell your drunk buddy "Uh oh, the chunky one who just walked in is ALREADY checking you out!" because when the mat-is-a-beepin' the dance floor-is-a-creakin'. Yes, the quantity of sex you have by pounds will go down, but in the long-run you'll thank us.

Sure it sounds shallow, but hey, you're the only guy on campus with his own Laser Light Show (pg. 174), you deserve to be picky.

The Fatty Detector Mat isn't only for parties. Set it up at your dorm room door and keep changing the settings as a mind-torture style fitness routine for your girlfriend. Everyone loves being told they're getting fat!

*Fat Chick Lure*

# Getting Started

Also detects small jackals, cars that are about to run into your house, people selling heavy stuff, and extremely large insects.

**Cost:**
$50

**Difficulty:**
Easier than getting a fatty to leave in the morning

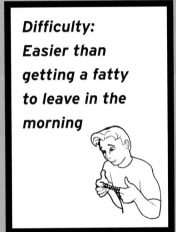

**Time:**
2 hours

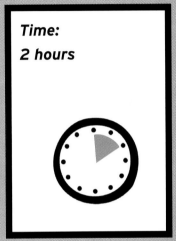

*Stuff You Need:*
- *Analog bathroom scale (with a mechanical dial)*
- *Electrical Microswitch (a switch with mounting holes).*
- *Plug in Lamp of some sort*
- *4 Sheet metal screws that fit though the mounting holes on the microswitch*
- *Electrical tape*

Are you tired of fatties ruining your parties? Want to prescreen your blind dates? The fatty detector is for you!

Are you a Fat Admirer (FA) or a chubby chaser? This project also can be right for you.

**1** First, decide on a weight threshold for your fatty detector. Depending on your taste in flesh, this can vary through the entire range of the weight scale you purchased.

**2** Once you've decided on your threshold, load down the scale to that weight. Bricks, a trashcan full of water, or an actual fat chick can all serve as a fine load.

**3** While the scale is weighted down appropriately, place a micro-switch on the side of the scale that doesn't move, in a position where the switch is activated.

Most scales have a top part that slides down over the bottom box, which sits on the ground. The micro-switch should be mounted to the bottom, non-moving box, in a position where when the top box moves down, it will trigger the switch.

**_Sample microswitches_**
**_with mounting holes_**

**4**

**5**

Most micro-switches click when they're activated. Place the switch in the correct position, and mark where the mounting holes should be.

Drill two holes in the side of the scale. Mount the switch with the sheet metal screws.

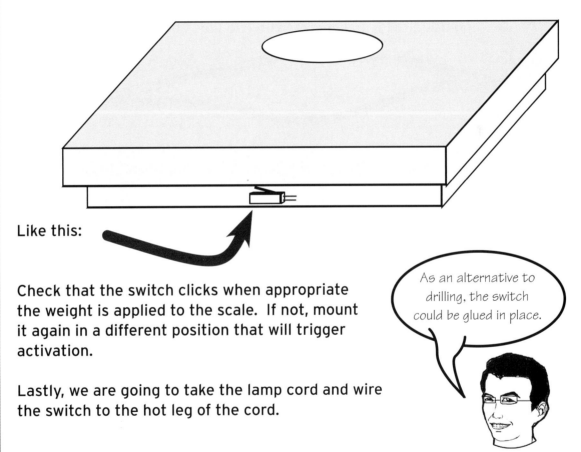

Like this:

**3**

Check that the switch clicks when appropriate the weight is applied to the scale. If not, mount it again in a different position that will trigger activation.

As an alternative to drilling, the switch could be glued in place.

Lastly, we are going to take the lamp cord and wire the switch to the hot leg of the cord.

*HELPFUL HINT: Fat chicks usually frequent buffets and other places that serve fried food, and can be lured onto the scale with a bucket of fried chicken. (Chocolate cake is a suitable alternative.)*

# 4

Next, take a typical lamp cord:

And use a razor to separate the two parts of the cord:

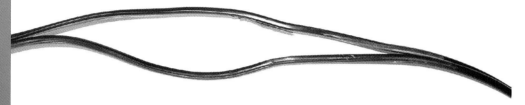

Trace back from the small prong on the plug to identify the "hot side" of the cord:

# 5

Once the hot side is identified, cut it.

**6** The hot cord from the plug should go to the terminal marked N.O. on the micro-switch. If the switch only has two terminals, just wire each side of the hot cord to a terminal. This can be done by soldering, by crimp connections, or just putting the wire though the hole in the switch terminal, and twisting it around.

**7** Then plug this bad boy in, and your lamp will turn on when the weight threshold is exceeded on the scale.

**8** Slide the scale under your doormat, and snake the wires under the door. The lamp will serve as your "Fatty Alert" system. When the light is lit, a fatty is standing outside your door.

Be sure to insulate this connection with the electrical tape.

Then sleep with the fatty you used to test the scale out. I know what you're thinking, but now that you have a Fatty Detector, this is the last time you'll be doing a heifer.

Might as well have one last hurrah.

Studies have proven this mat to be 95% more effective than placing a "Cow Crossing" sign in your window, but 20% less effective than mounting a harpoon gun over your door.

# How to Build An Internet Remote
## . . . For the High Tech Couch Potato

Since 1999, a majority of Americans have needed to surf the Internet in order to survive. From checking stocks to posting their favorite color on MySpace bulletins, there are a myriad of internet interactions everyone feels compelled to do in order to make it through any given hour.

A long time ago, people changed channels on their televisions by getting up and pressing a button on the console (they also bought record albums and paid to see movies...fools!) Anyhow, along with the advent of the TV remote control came other great progressions for society like microwave ovens, the mapping of the genome, and Duck Hunt.

*I just Googled myself.*

And now, we introduce the next great breakthrough in technology...

*A time machine with a Snoopy Sno Cone Machine attached, in case I want a Margarita in the future!?*

*No Dirty Mike, the Internet Remote Control.*

When you complete this project you'll be able to surf the internet from any vibrating couch or cardboard chair in the house. The Internet Remote Control will also come in handy in your bedroom; you'll no longer have to hover by your computer and manually close a browser window when someone unexpectedly walks in.

# Getting Started

**Cost:**
$50 - $200
It depends

**Difficulty:**
A PhD in patience and a few years experience as a computer programmer and an electrical engineer.

**Time:**
An hour to a week
It depends

**Stuff You Need:**
• It depends

The TV remote was invented by Robert Adler in 1956. If he was so smart, how come he didn'tinventtheInternet remote?

# WARNING

This project is for the super tech nerd.

The description is more an overview of what a techie could do to a remote when he's very, very bored. Exceptionally bored.

It's more a "too much time of your hands" kinda thing than "fun and games."

# Internet Remote

Wouldn't it be nice if you could just change the song on your computer as easy as you change a channel on TV?

Well then, you need the Internet Remote. If you think this is going to be complicated to program, you're correct. At least if you would like to do it cheaply.

You can skip all the complicated crap if you'd rather spend fifty bucks than solder a bunch of electrical components.

But if you want to go to the trouble of building an internet remote, this is how Jeremy would do it on the cheap:

I love my MP3 music collection so much I've wired every stereo in the house to play music from my computer. But it's a pain in the ass to walk all the way across the house when the computer randomly chooses a crappy song.

*Stuff You Need:*
- A Linux Music Server (Don't freak out if you're a Windows L0s3r, there is a windows version too)
- Serial Infrared Receiver (More about this below)
- Remote control:  Pretty much any remote control lying around your house will do.  You'll be able to use it for both your mp3s and your television, depending on where it's pointed.

*Software Needed:*
- XMMS Media Player (Who doesn't run XMMS?)
- LIRC (Linux Infrared Remote Control, get me at lirc.org)

## More about serial infrared receivers:

You can buy these pre-assembled, and some even come with a remote. Expect to pay around $50, but if you are lucky you will find one that comes with easy to use Windows software.

A simple serial port based receiver can be made for a couple of dollars. If you can use a soldiering iron, you can build this receiver:

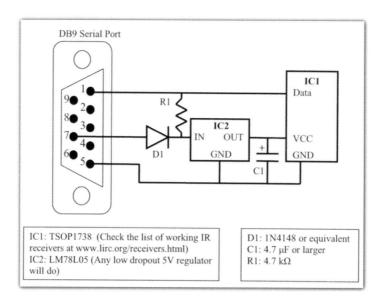

| DB9 Serial Port | | |
| --- | --- | --- |

IC1: TSOP1738 (Check the list of working IR receivers at www.lirc.org/receivers.html)
IC2: LM78L05 (Any low dropout 5V regulator will do)

D1: 1N4148 or equivalent
C1: 4.7 µF or larger
R1: 4.7 kΩ

For you people who still run Windows, a Windows version of WinLIRC can be obtained at winlirc.sourceforge.net.

This section is putting me to sleep. Would someone please turn the channel? And this page?

## Not so Advanced:

If you aren't adverse to spending money, this project can be expanded. Just buy what you need.

If you just want a way to skip songs remotely, I advise buying a PC remote that comes with its own software. Some newer, so called "media" PCs and certain video cards also come with remotes. Make sure to check the boxes that came with your computer.

Since you're already spending money here, you might as well get the best. I recommend a radio frequency (RF) remote, which will work at a range that will cover a decent-sized house, and doesn't need to be pointed in any particular direction.

The software included works fine for skipping songs on most music and video software. The really cool thing is: this remote control will also work with more advanced software, if you want to add more functionality later. (See the Advanced section.)

I use a Snapstream Firefly, and it works throughout my house. Elevate the antenna as far as possible for the best range. Learn more at: snapstream.com.

## Advanced:

Control audio visual equipment in your house with an IR transmitter (sometimes called an IR Blaster), that can both send IR signals, and allow a computer to control TV's and other A/V equipment.

Even better is a IR receiver/transmitter, which will allow you to both receive remote control signals, and control devices at the same time. The USB-UIRT is a very compatible IR receiver and transmitter, which you can get at usbuirt.com

## Super Advanced:

Lighting and appliances can be computer controlled by INSTEON or X-10 commands sent though a computer interface, including inside lighting, alarm systems, and thermostats. You'll need a computer interface for the standard being used, as well as control modules for each device under control.

Be sure to match the correct module to the application: use lamp modules for lights, appliance modules for appliances, motor modules for motors or inductive loads, and so forth. Remember not to use dimming light modules for florescent lights.

All kinds of modules exist, so you'll want to pick a standard and go with it. Try not to mix and match too many standards. X-10 is cheaper, but will not work in some areas due to noise on the electrical line. INSTEON is newer and more expensive but will be more reliable.

## Crazy Advanced:

If you have electrical experience, you can control high power loads by adding an addition relay. The appliance module would be wired to activate a relay, which in turn activates a high powered device, or an air conditioner. I control the Jacuzzi pump and heater with my internet remote.

Get a relay with coils designed for 110V AC, or a DC adapter will be necessary between the module and the relay.

Relays will have two sets of ratings: One will be a voltage and a current to switch the relay. The second rating will indicate how large a load or device that the relay can switch. The power load of the relay should be larger than the load to be controlled. With a 220V load, the relay should have two contacts, because both phases to the load need to be switched.

**See below:**

Okay Jeremy, we get it. You're smart.

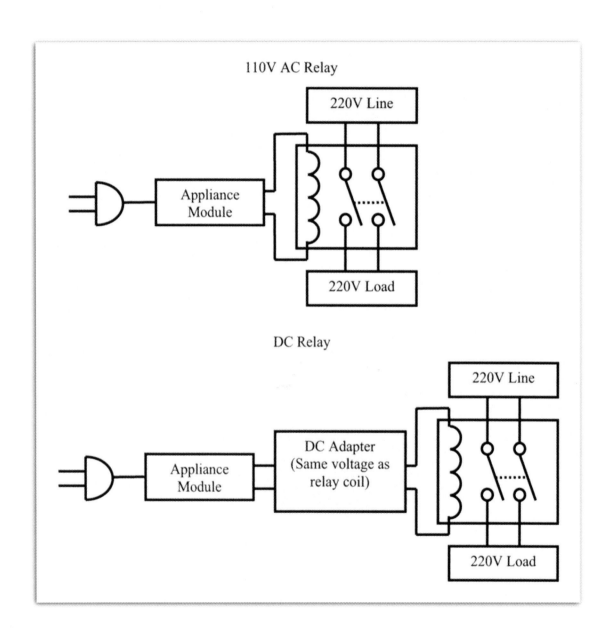

## *Software for the Advanced Projects:*

All software should work together. There are many software packages for home/audio/visual automation: I use software called Girder, which can coordinate IR remotes, Firefly, X-10, INSTEON, computer functions, internet, web server, home theater, and more. I'm still figuring out how to do even more with this setup, you'll find tons of documentation and examples at girder.nl.

I'm running Linux but the config file for LIRC doesn't support the receiver I built? Any suggestions?

Show me your boobs.

# How to Build
# A Water Balloon Launcher
## ... To Put Out Local Fires

Twelve-year-olds getting off of a school bus. A grandmother carrying a bag of groceries. A puppy watching a video of an otter petting a dolphin. All great targets for latex spheres of water.

> Well this is a relief. My brain still itches from trying to read the last chapter.

Water Balloons never lose their charm. For many reasons the frequency of buying them tends to go down as your life progresses, but fill up a bucket of those babies and you're always guaranteed good times.

After throwing around blobs of rubber-encased water for years on end, you may wonder about ways to increase the number of people you can hit with a liquidy assault. That's why we developed a Water Balloon Launcher! Had one as a kid? Not like this! The Super Power Balloon Launcher you're about to make will not only shoot faster, farther and more accurately, it will also cost you less than the wimpy kid models.

# Getting Started

**Cost:**
$25

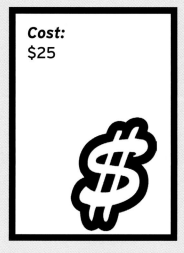

**Difficulty:**
Splash...

**Time:**
1 hour

**Stuff You Need:**
- Around 20 feet of stretchy latex surgical tubing
- Large funnel
- Small section of rope
- Possibly Necessary: a metal ring, or large washer that doesn't fit through the funnel exit

Your water balloon launcher is going to need three people to launch it, so start making friends.

A Super-Power Water Balloon Launcher is basically a glorified slingshot, powered by three people.

These things are great for launching water balloons, rotten fruit, snowballs, and anything else that doesn't fit, or is too delicate for shooting from a Potato Cannon (see next section.)

**1** Drill four holes in the funnel, sized slightly larger than the diameter of the tubing.

**2** Cut the length of tubing in half, and thread each through two holes in the funnel. Tie ends of the tubing together to create two loops.

**3** Take the small section of rope, and tie it in a small loop though the metal ring / washer. Thread the end of the rope though the funnel exit, creating a handle.

## *Launching Crap:*

**4** This should be obvious, but you need two people, or something like two trees to hold the loops of tube. Put something in the funnel, pull back and let go.

> **TIP**
> *You should probably use the Balloon Launcher to lob fun surprises, like candy or confetti or Molotov cocktails.*

Be careful, as launching rocks can break ribs...

**Funnel
(Top View)**

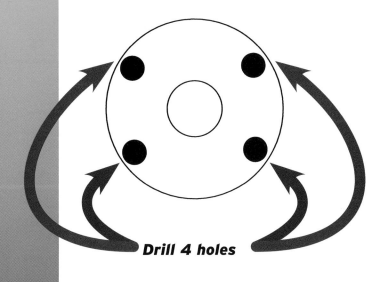

Drill 4 holes

**Side View
(Not to scale)**

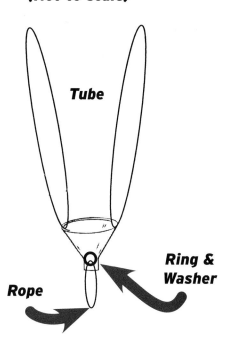

Tube

Ring &
Washer

Rope

**GUINNESS
WORLD RECORD:**
The world's biggest
water balloons are
inside Kelly Pickler's
chest.

If you build one of these,
you are legally a firefighter
in Kentucky.

# How to Build
# A Potato Gun
## . . . Stop Kitchen Invasions!

As you know, sitting down to a state dinner with international enemies can be tense. It helps to have the confidence that you could defend yourself with the hors d'oeuvres you find in front of you. Thus, your dire need for a high-velocity Potato Gun.

> This section is complicated as fuck. It's not like the others. Prepare yourself.

Let's be honest about a brutal truth: potatoes have had it way too easy. They've enjoyed sitting around unmolested while pranksters seized and abused every other food product, from eggs to soap. Time to include potatoes in your devastating plans against your arch-enemies and nerdier business associates. The police would thank you, if they weren't too busy dodging bullets fired by bad guys who aren't polite enough to use a potato gun.

FYI, this section is much more informational than "How-To." We could write an entire book on building potato guns. There is something eternally cool about building something that can launch a projectile faster than a human can throw.

> I only wanted to do this section so I could show off my potato guns.

But despite the name, these devices aren't limited to potatoes. We've cannoned lemons, oranges, tennis balls, T-shirts, toilet paper, and even small pumpkins.

Prepare for some nerdy background info.

I find this chapter very offensive.

A modified potato gun once broke the speed of sound. The next day, 400 banks were robbed in Idaho.

# Compressed Air Cannons

For normal-sized cannons (barrels less than six feet long and weighing less than 100 lbs.), the compressed air versions are more powerful and safer, but harder to build.

Compressed air cannons either require an air compressor, or need to be pumped up by a bicycle tire pump.

Compressed air cannons can fire things like t-shirts (and other flammable stuff, such as rolls of toilet paper) without fire damage to the projectiles.

## Combustion Cannons

For normal sized cannons, combustion cannons are more portable, and do not require the use of an air compressor. They tend to be more finicky than compressed air cannons, and the power of a particular shot can vary quite a bit, especially when using an aerosol-can-based propellant.

Combustion cannons can also be dangerous when used with powerful or fast burning fuels, i.e. welding gasses such as hydrogen, MAPP or Acetylene.

Taken to the extreme, combustion cannons can vastly outperform compressed air cannons. Due to the laws of physics, breaking the sound barrier with compressed air is not possible without the use of difficult techniques.

Combustion cannons can be scaled to the supersonic and beyond, if you know the engineering behind them. These cannons are extremely dangerous and loud.

But they are a ton of fun.

# WARNING

If it wasn't obvious from the above, potato cannons can be dangerous so don't build them, unless you are an engineer (or have one to work on this with you). You are not as smart as Jeremy.

# Simple Combustion Cannon

Basic Theory

A simple combustion cannon is just a couple pieces of pipe from your local hardware store put together, with some sort of ignition method in the combustion chamber. The potato is loaded in the barrel of the gun, and then propellant (usually hairspray) is sprayed into the combustion chamber. The chamber is then sealed, and the ignition system causes the gas in the chamber to ignite, and push the potato out of the barrel.

---

**Materials Needed:**
- 2 to 3 feet of 2" ABS pressure pipe
- 1 foot of 4" ABS pressure pipe
- ABS Cement (ABS pipe glue)
- Lantern lighter
- 4" to 2" reducing fitting
- 4" Cleanout fitting with threaded cap (a threaded end with a plug)

---

Assemble the cannon as show below:

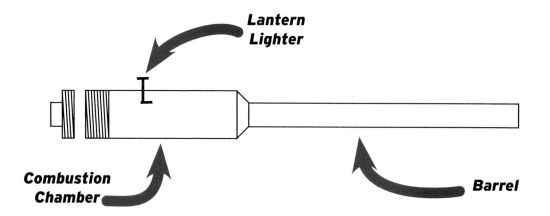

**Lantern Lighter**

**Combustion Chamber**

**Barrel**

Drill a hole, sized for the lantern lighter, in the 4″ ABS about half way down. Install the lantern lighter in the hole. Next, assemble the fittings together with the ABS glue.

It will help to sharpen the edges of the end of the barrel. This will help in loading uncut potatoes. (See the Potato Cutter section if interested in precutting potatoes.)

Launching Procedure:

> Your mother says:
>
> > Never point these things at people, and don't look down the barrel.

1.  Cut a potato in half lengthwise (optional)
2.  Unscrew top of cannon
3.  Jam the potato down the barrel with a broomstick
4.  Spray some fuel into the chamber
5.  Screw cap in place
6.  Aim at something safe
7.  Give the lantern lighter a twist.

## *Fuel Types*

Many types of fuels can be used in a Potato Cannon, some with better results than others, and some dangerous. Any flammable aerosol deodorants or hair spray will work, but will gunk up the potato cannon with the residue they leave behind. Companies constantly change the formulation of their products, so specific products will not be discussed.

Butane lighter refills burn very cleanly but can be tough when it comes to measuring out the right amount by hand. Starting Fluid from an automotive supply house has the same issues. Propane is probably the best all-round fuel, and can be metered by using an unlit propane pencil torch.

Gasses to avoid in a plastic gun include: pure oxygen, MAPP gas, hydrogen, and acetylene will cause explosions that plastic pipe can't handle, and you'll end up holding a large plastic bomb.

Rapid repeated firing will not work well, making your projectile not fire very far, unless the chamber has time to clear the smoke and replenish the oxygen supply.

## *Improvements on this basic design include:*

1. Using a connector between the barrel and the chamber, such as a camlock to increase loading time, and creating a system of interchangeable barrels.

2. Using a small computer fan to speed combustion chamber clearing time.

3. Electronic ignition, using BBQ spark lighter, a electronic stun gun, or a coil out of a car.

4. A fuel metering system to get the correct mixture, can be as simple as a fuel bottle attached to a series of two valves, with the correct length of pipe in between.

### What type of pipe to use?

Hardware stores typically carry various types of PVC and ABS plastic pipe, copper and assorted steel metal pipes. Metal pipes are overkill for your basic potato guns, so we'll skip these for now.

Even I know that.

Combustion can be a violent process, generating heat and shock. The chosen pipe will need to stand up to this...and not explode.

You don't want your spud gun to explode. The chosen pipe should also fail safely, and not send out shrapnel.

| AMMO | BARREL SIZE |
|------|-------------|
| Potato | 1.5", 2" |
| Tennis Balls | 2.5" |
| Rolled T-shirts, plastic soda bottles, under-filled water balloons, oranges | 3" |

## Types of pipe:

**PVC**

White plastic sprinkler pipe, is what most people are familiar with, and will probably be the first type of pipe encountered in a hardware store.
BUT DO NOT USE PVC PIPE FOR COMBUSTION CANNONS.

It will be tempting, because PVC usually has the best selection of fittings and such. But PVC is brittle and inflexible compared to ABS pipe: PVC tends to tear and break, while ABS tends to deform.  Also, PVC doesn't stand up well to heat,  which means that a PVC cannon is more likely to explode, and if it does, it's more likely to create plastic shrapnel which can cause injury.

**ABS**

This black plastic pipe has a variety of uses, but you're looking for the pressure rated solid wall (not cellular core) schedule 40 ABS pipe.  Pipe thickness is specified in schedule.  Schedule 80 is even better, but hard to find.

# Simple Compressed Air Cannon

**Materials:**

- 1″ Ball Valve
  (Threaded Metal)

- 4 Feet of 2″ ABS pressure pipe
  (Other sizes will work, see Ammo/Barrel Discussion)

- 2 Feet of  4″ ABS pressure pipe

- 4″ to 1″ Threaded adapter
  (You might need to use a combination of adapters to achieve this)

- 4″ End cap

- 2″ (or whatever barrel size you're using) to 1″ Threaded adapter

- Schrader valve
  (a car tire inflation valve)

- ABS glue

- Thread compound
  (Optional)

**Hero Remembered
Ronald McDonald
1965-2001**

Spokesperson and mascot of
McDonald's restaurants.

Killed with a potato gun by the Hamburglar in a
botched armed robbery.

**1** Attach all of the fittings according to the following diagram:

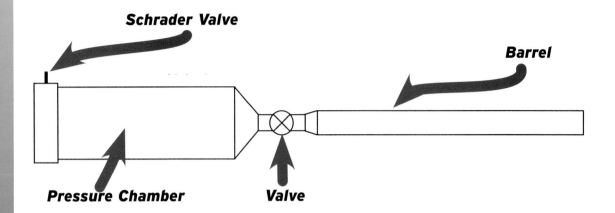

**Schrader Valve**

**Barrel**

**Pressure Chamber**       **Valve**

**2** The thread compound is most important on the threaded seal between the valve and the pressure tank. You don't want pressure leaking out while you're pumping it up. Apply to the male threads pretty liberally, and a bit less to the female threads: don't gunk up the ball valve with excess thread compound.

**3** Glue all of the slip fittings with ABS glue. Make sure the fittings fit well, and remove all burrs with a knife. Apply glue to both ends, and push together with a quarter turn twist. Hold together for a few seconds to set, as sometimes they tend to come apart.

**4** Drill a hole in the end, or the side of the end cap for the Schrader valve, and insert. If the valve is loose in the hole, some glue can be used. Dry overnight for safety.

# A Sprinkler valve with a Trigger

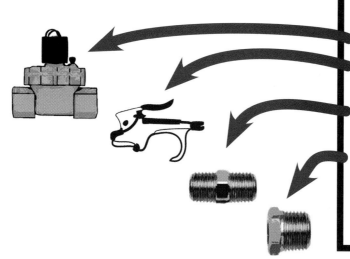

### Additional Parts Necessary:

- 1" Electronic Sprinkler Valve
- Blowgun for Air Compressor (optional)
- 1/4" NPT Nipple (preferably hex)
- 1/4" to 3/8" reducer bushing (Possibly necessary)
- 1/4" 90 degree Street Ell (Nice, but not necessary)

Use the sprinkler valve in place of the ball valve. Make sure to get the direction correct: There's an arrow, which should be pointing toward the barrel. There are two ways to actuate this valve: the ghetto way, leaves the valve intact, and it easy.  Just use the manual actuation screw to fire the gun.  In case you didn't know where that is, here is a pic:

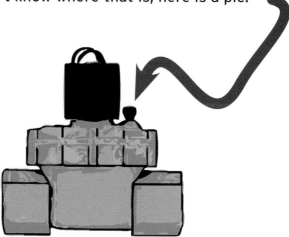

The second way involves modifying the sprinkler valve to actuate with a blowgun, which is the ideal method. But we won't be covering it in detail, mostly because this section is already horribly unfunny, and there are a billion articles on the Internet about modding sprinkler valves for use in spud guns.

The basic steps are: Take apart the valve, and plug the bypass hole with glue. The bypass hold is the on the output side of the valve: a little tube with a hole in it.  Remove the electric solenoid, and thread in the blowgun. You may need to use the 1/4" to 3/8" reducer bushing, depending on the size of the thread of the solenoid.  Using the 90 degree street ell will allow the blowgun to be more of a trigger, rather than sticking straight out of the potato gun.

As a last note, it's possible to use an electronic trigger by wiring a switch to the solenoid to two nine volt batteries in series.  If you don't know what the means, research on the goddamn Internet. Series circuits aren't funny at all, seriously.

# Breech Loader

A breech loader can increase loading fun. No more jamming shit all the way down the barrel. Just place in the breech, and slide closed.

*1*

Find a tube that slides over the pipe easily. In the below photos, we've used a hybrid of both 1.5" and 2" pipe over each other for extra strength, because the cut-out weakens the PVC a lot.

*2*

Notice how the both ends of the breech are supported in my design: two inch exhaust tubing slides really well over two inch PVC pipe. An O-ring can be used for extra performance, but isn't necessary, if you mill a notch in the outer PVC pipe with a small spin cutter, or rotary tool. The depth is fairly hard to get right, so I use a scrap piece of PVC pipe, and keep trying until it's correct.

Some people have also had good luck making breech loaders using PVC slide (telescopic) repair couplings from the hardware stores. These are PVC joints that expand to repair broken sections of pipe without digging up the entire length of pipe.

**TIP**

It's necessary to shape the ammo beforehand, if you're using a breech loader. Fortunately, this is easy. Just cut a small piece of PVC pipe left over from your barrel, and sharpen the edges. Use this to carve a potato on the cutting board, and you will have perfectly shaped potato ammo every time.

## BONUS INFO

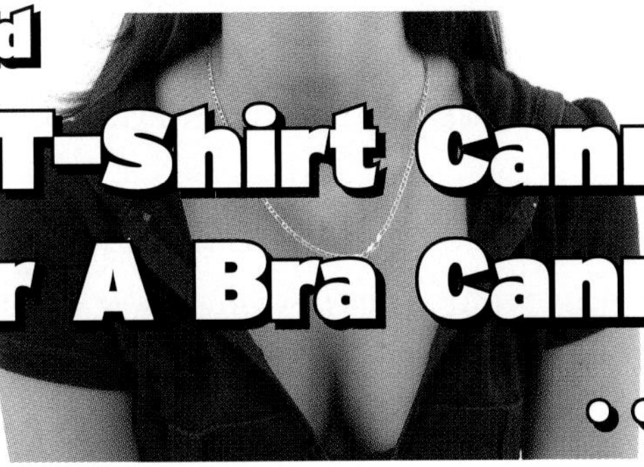

# How to Build
# A T-Shirt Cannon,
# Or A Bra Cannon
## . . . or whatever

Follow steps 1 through 50 of the How to Build a Potato Gun section and then do the following:

**1**

Insert t-shirt, bra, or whatever.

Hey, I can do this one!

**2**

Fire!!!

# How to Build
# A Toilet Paper Cannon
## ... For Apartment Buildings

If you have friends who live in apartment buildings, who miss out on the fun of being TPed, this variation on the Potato Gun is for you. You can TP up to a six story building with a pneumatic Toilet Paper Cannon.

This won't be a step-to-step guide, but assumes you have built a few cannons and know what you are doing. We aren't going to discuss anything but the barrel, because the other parts are no different from other compressed air cannons. If I have to tell you why this cannon needs to be pneumatic (compressed air) this project isn't for you.

Why?

Think about it. Because the TP would come out burning from a combustion cannon.

Most TP cannons are equipped with a large enough barrel, to fit a standard TP roll endwise, which is actually pretty lame, because the paper should unroll as it flies for proper draping action. Also, loading the paper endwise requires the user to plug the cardboard center of the roll.

We've designed a square barrel, loaded the TP sideways rather than endwise, and add some sandpaper on one side of the barrel to impart a nice spin in order to unroll the toilet paper.

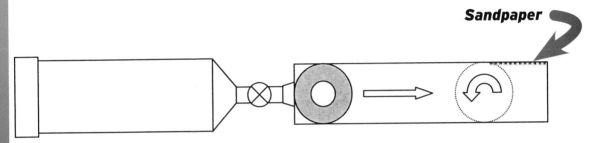

**Sandpaper**

This square barrel can be made from metal, or wood, but the easiest material to work with is medium-density fiberboard (MDF). However, MDF isn't very strong and flat surfaces tend to bow and crack under high pressure. The sides of the square barrel are several square feet, and under low pressure, say 10 psi, the force on the wood will be over a ton.

Under such forces, it is necessary that we reinforce the square barrel. Hose clamps work well, but we cannot just wrap hose clamps around a square barrel. We need to wrap hose clamps around a circular surface. In order to accomplish this reinforcement, we will construct four small arches made out of MDF. We will place these arches around the square barrel as seen in the following diagram:

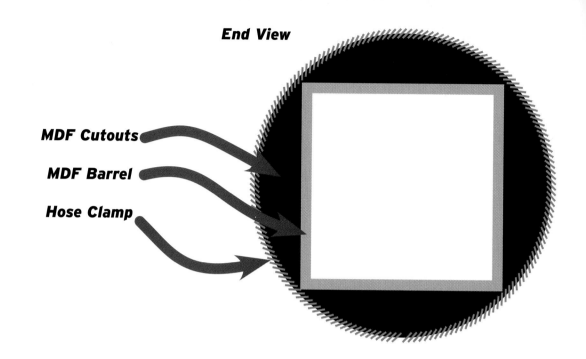

**MDF Cutouts**

**MDF Barrel**

**Hose Clamp**

**Supports every few inches**

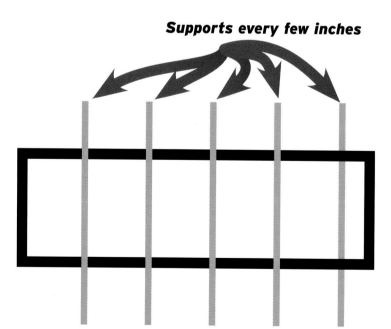

**Side View**

These supports will be necessary every few inches. Plan to make one circular support for every four inches of barrel length. Start by cutting circles out of MDF and then cut out a barrel sized rectangular hole in the exact center of each circle. Then, cut the remainder of the circles into four pieces like in the diagram. Place these pieces around the barrel and hold them in place with a large hose clamp.

## HISTORY COMES ALIVE!

Russians first invented the TP cannon in 1867, but abandoned the project when they could not find any toilet paper.

### BELIEVE IT OR FUCK OFF!

In 1967, Meredith Quigley accidentally sat on a loaded toilet paper cannon, causing it to fire. Because of this tragic event, Meredith Quigley hasn't had to wipe her ass for over 40 years.

### BELIEVE IT OR FUCK OFF!

# How to Build
# A Gravity Bong
## ... You know, for Smoking, Umm, Tobacco

Green tobacco was created so that humans could commune with Mother Nature, and achieve a form of spiritual enlightenment.

Experts say there's no better way to do this than by huffing a giant bongload and giggling on your bathroom floor for three hours.

Seriously, this is a potent device, considering how cheap it is to make. Historians say Pythagoras first conceived of the gravity bong when he got in a bathtub and realized he wasn't high.

So, the gravity bong represents 1,000 years of hydraulic evolution at your fingertips, and you should appreciate that. But you won't remember that in ten minutes, anyway, so whatever.

Who knew that a little gravity could get you so baked?

# Getting Started

**Cost:**
**Less than $10**

**Difficulty:**
**Depends on how high on "tobacco" you are**

**Time:**
**15 minutes**

Be careful not to heat the plastic cap. If that got you high, you wouldn't need "tobacco."

**Stuff You Need:**
- 1-gallon plastic bottle*
- Scissors
- A bowl from an old pipe

*For the gangster version, use a 5-gallon water bottle

You'll probably want to add a few burritos to the materials list.

**1** Start by cutting the bottom off of the bottle.

You should probably use a knife to cut the bottom off if you're choosing the 5-gallon jug.

**2** Then poke a hole in the bottle cap big enough for the bowl.

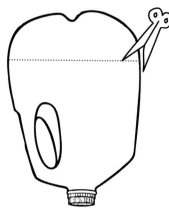

Then screw in the bowl, duh.

**3** Next, place the bottle into a bucket of water.

# 4

Light the bowl and pull up on the bottle as you do to let smoke in.

# 5

Then remove the cap and push the bottle down, while breathing in.

Holy crap, that smoke was hot!

Well, then turn the page.

## *How it Works*

- The Gravity Bong uses gravity to create a vacuum that sucks smoke into the bottle.

- Bring up "vacuums" after smoking a few bowls, and we bet it'll stir up some stimulating conversation (but then again, so would a pretty rock).

# Ice Cooled Smoke

If you use two containers that fit inside of each other for the bong you can put ice between them to keep the bowl cool.

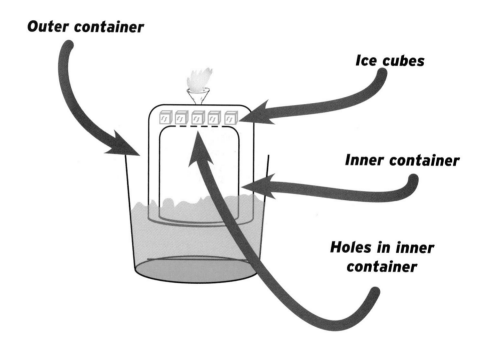

**Outer container**

**Ice cubes**

**Inner container**

**Holes in inner container**

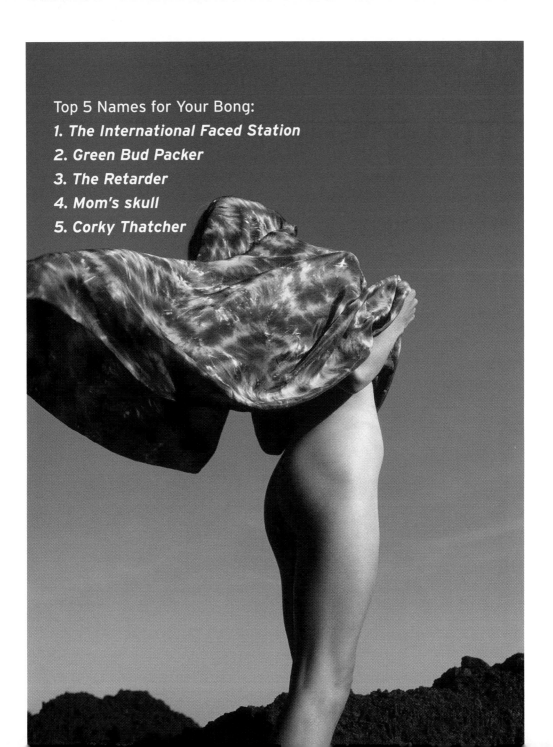

Top 5 Names for Your Bong:

1. *The International Faced Station*
2. *Green Bud Packer*
3. *The Retarder*
4. *Mom's skull*
5. *Corky Thatcher*

# Also from National Lampoon Press

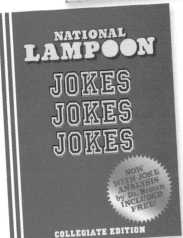

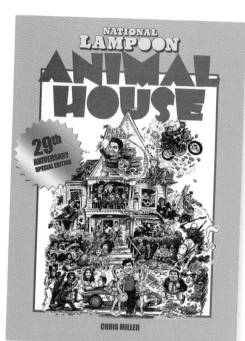

NATIONAL LAMPOON
ANIMAL HOUSE
29th ANNIVERSARY SPECIAL EDITION
CHRIS MILLER

NATIONAL LAMPOON®
HELP!
Self-Help for the Selfish Helpless!
finance,
sex,
dating,
and health...
HELP!!!
Scott Rubin

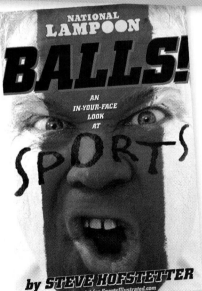

NATIONAL LAMPOON
BALLS!
AN IN-YOUR-FACE LOOK AT
SPORTS
by STEVE HOFSTETTER
Columnist for SportsIllustrated.com

Guaranteed to insult EVERYONE!
NATIONAL LAMPOON®
JOKES
JOKES
JOKES
VERBAL ABUSE EDITION
Steve Ochs

NATIONAL LAMPOON®
ROAD TRIP USA
ALL THE PLACES YOUR DAD NEVER STOPPED AT
by Harmon Leon

# NATIONAL LAMPOON's BAG BOY

## The competitive sport of grocery bagging needs a hero.

"Very, very funny script. Fresh and original."

Peter & Bobby Farrelly (Something About Mary, Shallow Hal, Dumb & Dumber)

www.nationallampoon.com